DITKA

An Autobiography

Mike Ditka
with Don Pierson

Bonus Books, Chicago

90   89   88   87   86   5

Library of Congress Catalog Card Number: 86-70706

International Standard Book Number: 0-933-89307-8

Bonus Books, Inc.
160 East Illinois Street
Chicago, Illinois 60611

Printed in the United States of America

This is dedicated to George Halas, and to Gale Sayers, Dick Butkus, Brian Piccolo and all the other great Bears who couldn't be part of the 1985 world championship season.

—Mike Ditka

Contents

FROM LANDRY TO HALAS

HEAD COACH

PROFILES

STRAIGHT TALK

Foreword

This book, more than a story of a football coach and his team, is the story of a man and his relationship to life.

I found Mike's story intriguing from the standpoint of a person's growth through the whole experience of pro football. The player who came to us in 1969 was not as good a man as the coach who won the Super Bowl seventeen years later.

Mike started out at the top as a player on those great Bears' teams of the early 60s. By the end of the decade, the Bears had fallen on hard times and so had Ditka. I saw Mike begin to work his way back with us, first as a player and then as a coach. When George Halas called him back to Chicago, Mike and the Bears were ready to climb the ladder together.

The book is very revealing of the relationships between coaches and players. It has rare insight on the thought processes of both groups, and the way they can work together toward a common goal.

Mike's opinions here are spontaneous, and they're his. Ditka doesn't waste time trying to present himself as something he's not, either in print or face to face.

Although I cannot condone the use of four-letter words in this book or elsewhere, I can endorse the book's Christian intent.

Finally, understand that the Super Bowl victory, and this autobiography, are simply milestones on the Christian road that Mike Ditka has chosen and on which he is making a successful—if sometimes bumpy—journey.

It's a good story, and the best is yet to come.

—*Tom Landry*
Head Coach
Dallas Cowboys

May 1986

SUPER

I

Don't You Like Me?

We were leading Seattle 7-0. It was the fourth game of the 1984 season and we were undefeated. We had taken the ball right up the field on the Seahawks. We took the ball again and ran it. It was second and 5. I got Walter Payton averaging 5.7 yards a carry at that point. The call, it was a great play, a little bit of a trick play. We were going to run a slant with two guys leading Walter.

Bob Avellini had started at quarterback because Jim McMahon was hurt. I was standing there looking. Ed Hughes, our offensive coordinator, is beside me and Ed said, "Oh-oh."

I said, "What? What?"

I said, "We'll make the first down and go right down and kick these guys' asses!"

Ed said, "Oh-oh, he's audibling!"

I said, "Oh no, don't do that."

As soon as he audibled, our receiver, Dennis McKinnon, shifted. The Seattle guy shifted off of Dennis. Avellini threw the ball. The Seattle guy caught the ball on the dead run and ran for a touchdown.

I couldn't believe it. I couldn't even get mad at him. I was so shocked and I was so pissed off I couldn't get mad.

I said, "Bob, why would you do that? Don't you like me?"

Nobody loves the Bears any more than I do. I don't care who it is. There's nobody. I know what my feelings are. Not only that, I love the city. I think the city has been so much maligned. It's a great city with great people. I don't always agree with the fans. I don't always agree with the politics of the city, but it's a great mixture of a lot of things. It's a city that can do anything it wants to do if it wants to do it.

Winning the Super Bowl was something I saw myself doing. I think you see yourself certain places in life. I saw myself in New Orleans winning the Super Bowl. I told people at a speech in the spring of 1985 at the Westminster Bank in New York that I wanted to be the first coach who played in a Super Bowl in New Orleans and won, was an assistant coach in a Super Bowl in New Orleans and won, and head coach in a Super Bowl in New Orleans and won. I said, "It's going to happen." If it wouldn't have happened, those people would have said, "That guy was crazy."

It's all part of the master plan, or whatever you want to call it. I'm not sure we shouldn't have won it in 1984. I don't care how good the San Francisco 49ers were. I had a lot to do with screwing that up. I got too conservative instead of going out and attacking. Getting as close as we did could have given us a fat head in 1985, but we went out and worked even though we had some injuries and some holdouts. That's why I think we can go back in 1986. Our guys are going to go back and work. I think we have a lot of Grabowskis.

I had more fun looking at O'Bradovich and Butkus the night after the Super Bowl, crying—Marconi, Bishop, Fortunato, Abe Gibron, all the old guys. I think you do things for yourself in life, but if I want to say one thing, this was for the past. It's for the present, because those are the guys who did it, but it's really for the past. Even though some of the old guys played on championship teams in the 40s, like Sid Luckman and the Osmanskis, I would think this has to be very exciting for them to see a rebirth of what they experienced as players themselves and understand the Bears have become the talk of the town and country, just like they were.

I was really happy for the fans, all the fans. I get letters from die-hard Cub fans who have now become true-blue Bear fans. I got letters of congratulations from the other managers in the other sports. We broke the jinx. The fans always have been good fans. Sometimes fans think they're fans and they're really goofballs who got a ticket from somebody and want to be a pain in the ass because they had six drinks. But I get letters from housewives, from kids, and I think they're the true fans. They say, "You don't know how great you made my winter. You don't know how great you made my fall. My husband is in a better mood than he's been in ever." To me, that is what's worthwhile. It's not pleasing the guy who has six bucks bet on the game and has some drinks in him and all of a sudden he's going to tell you what you did wrong.

I have to remind myself this is all just a kid's game. I say it because it was meant to be a sport and meant to be fun. But it's a business. I just hope I never become so callous to say that I'm in this job because it's a good living and that's why I enjoy it. That's bullshit. If I ever said that, I think I'd walk out of the job. It becomes more than a game because it's your life. You get wrapped up in it. You get wrapped up in the winning and losing and wrapped up in the fans, the disappointments and the joys. You hear people time and again saying, "I can't tell you how proud we were." Or, "I can't tell you how disappointed we were." You realize a big part of their life revolves around what happens every Sunday afternoon. Maybe it shouldn't be that way, but it is that way.

As far back as 1977 when Jack Pardee left the Bears to coach the Redskins, I had people call me to ask if I was interested. I'd tell them I wasn't ready for the job. In the back of my mind, I thought someday I'd like to coach the Bears, but I said I wasn't ready. I wasn't looking to be a head coach anyplace. When jobs opened in Atlanta, L.A., Denver, or anywhere else, I'm sure they weren't interested in me, but I sure wasn't interested in them either. That's the truth. I don't know why. I really don't.

I really feel there has been an interesting cycle in my life that's been laid out and it's supposed to happen that way. I just think God places people in life and then he places other people in their lives to give them direction or to change their direction. If you really think of it, it's really amazing that I'm in Chicago, period. Totally amazing. It's amazing because of the circumstances of my leaving when I was a player and the way I came back. It was of my own doing when I left. I could have stopped it, but I didn't. I cried when I left.

As big a hunk as the Cowboys took out of my life and as much as the Cowboys gave to me, I'm still a Bear. It's that simple. I was never an Eagle. That was a fleeting moment to get me back on the ground, get me back to basics. The Cowboys picked up the pieces and put them together. When they got together, I was a Bear. I really believe that.

When I started coaching in Dallas under Tom Landry, I was always accused of being a Bear. He would say, "You're too basic. You've got that Bear philosophy."

About the last three years I was there, I really started feeling itchy and wanted to try something and be on my own. It never became an obsession. But it became something I thought about a lot more.

People said, "You can't do this. You couldn't do that. You shouldn't do this." Vince Lombardi was just a poor high school coach. Then he went to West Point. Then he went to the Giants. Then he went to the Packers.

Whatever you are, you are. You're a person who deals with people and it's how you deal with them that counts. I think there's a big fallacy about coaching. They want to say it's X's and O's. It isn't X's and O's. There are qualified high school coaches who can tell you about X's and O's and the 34 defense or two-deep zones. What good does it get you? Coaching is people. It's being able to put your philosophy in place and being able to attack with it, to have ways to get it done.

I don't profess to be any better or any worse than anybody else. You have to have people help you. You've got to have good assistants, a good management team, a good scouting team, and good players. That's what makes it work. There has to be a guy to hold the puzzle together, but you have to have other people around you to help. I think as good a coach as Tom Landry is, he always has pretty good assistants.

I was a Cowboy, but I was still more Bear. I loved the Cowboys. I was excited about it. I was there when that city was just growing, when they were becoming America's Team or whatever it is. That was fun. It was a tremendous thing to be involved in five Super Bowls with a team. Think about it. Poor Mike Ditka traded to the Eagles, going to get bounced out of football, gets traded to the Cowboys and gets to two Super Bowls, plays in one, starts the other, catches a TD pass, coaches in three. Incredible when you stop to think about it. And you think things don't happen for reasons?

Do the players like me? I doubt that very many of them like me, but I can't worry about that. That's the least of my worries. But I like them.

When things are going well, they like you. If things are going bad, they don't. They find a way to point the finger. That's life. That's the animal. When things go bad, they find things wrong with a lot of people. Everybody does.

I heard some of the players called me Sybil, like the book about the lady who had all those personality changes. Doesn't bother me. I can call a lot of players Sybil, too. I see a lot of personality changes out there. I even see courage changes. Doesn't bother me. Players have a right to call me anything they want. My whole waking, sleeping, living and dying is not based on what a player thinks about me. But it is important that he produces and does his job to the best of his ability within the system. Yeah, you hope they all like you, but then that's impossible anyways. I was thinking about that not too long ago. Thinking back to the Old Man, George Halas. Thinking back to Landry. Back to my high school coach, Carl Aschman. I had great respect for them, but as far as liking them all the time, that was never true. You never always agree with the philosophy of the coach. You don't always want to work when he says work. I probably was a little flighty my first couple years here. I don't question them calling me the Three Faces of Eve, or Sybil, or whatever it was. How many games did we play? I had a face for each game.

I don't think it's a secret that everything in life is based on people. There's a sign in my office that says one word: "Communication." I don't always do the best job of that, but I know it's the most important thing you can do. The first year I was here, when I hollered at someone on the sideline, all hell broke loose. What the hell? Why should hell break loose? Hell doesn't break loose when I pat 'em on the ass after they make the good play. Why should it break loose when you holler at somebody? Well, they said, they're not used to that. Well, that's tough. That's really unusual. They're not used to winning, either. They're not used to doing the right thing. Yeah, I hollered at some guys on the sideline when I was in Dallas, too. They hollered back at me. But I hollered back at them, too, if they weren't doing what the hell we worked on. But what really baffled me when I came here was that guys' skin was so thin. I mean what the hell's going on? You want to get better or you want to stay the same? And I know there is a lot of advice on criticism. If you're going to praise somebody, do it in public; if you're going to criticize, do it over the phone. I've heard all that crap. I think that's probably true, but I just think I've never been unfair to somebody as far as applauding when they've done something right and I also don't think I've been overly critical.

There were times when I got so damn mad that first year because we couldn't even line up in the right formation. In our first game in 1982, we looked like a bunch of idiots. Should have won the game going away. Got beat 17-10.

I don't condone by any means a lot of things I do. I don't accept them as being right. But I accept them as being me and I know I'm capable of changing and getting better. I don't say they're right or wrong. I don't say they're the right example. I know that sometimes we don't always do what we want to do, but that can be changed in time as long as you think about it and understand and work on it and do something about it. If you don't care about it and it doesn't bother you, then I think you have a problem.

I'm getting better about getting mad at players. But damn, it's important to do your job. If you're a football player and you miss a critical play or get a critical penalty that costs us a chance to score or a chance to win the game, it's important. Here's what it would be like: Supposing I was a welder building a skyscraper. I say, "This looks pretty good to me. I'm going to leave out this steel girder. I just won't put it in." When the building goes up, all of a sudden it caves in because I left something out.

That's what it amounts to. If it's your job, do it. The guy has to put all the bolts in the right places or it doesn't work. Concentration in doing your job is so important. I just don't buy all the excuses that are made. "Well, we'll get 'em the next time."

I like to talk about Bear football. To me, Bear football can be described this way: "Ask no quarter, give no quarter." I just think you play the game within the rules and don't ask for anything. That's true of everything you do in life. That's golf, anything.

I kind of get a little nervous, no, I don't get nervous, I get mad, when I see these guys on a football field always patting each other on the ass. That bothers me. When the game starts, shake his hand and wish him good luck, and when the game's over, congratulate him and get out of there. But I don't understand all this fraternizing. That guy is trying to take food out of your mouth. He's trying to take money out of your bank. I don't understand it. I really saw it in 1982 when they were going through that strike. It became sickening. They were hugging. You see it more now than you ever saw it when we played. During the game, just play. Tennis players aren't shaking hands during the game. Golf players aren't. Shake before. Shake after. Let's play.

You know what bothered me most about the 1985 season? Did anyone happen to look out in the Orange Bowl an hour and a half before the Miami game? A lot of our players were out there and a lot of their players were out there and everybody's playing grab ass. We're patting; they're patting. Hey, this is football. You don't do that stuff. So what if they think you're a lousy, no-good rat. That's life. Shake his hand after the game. You don't see boxers go around grabbing ass before they fight, do you?

We play hard. I think the fans relate to that more than anything. A guy said to me, "I've been a fan for 30 years. The main thing that griped me was when you only had five guys on the team that were really breaking their asses." I said, "I don't see that anymore."

I think that's what we've tried to establish. That's the kind of football we want to play, tough and aggressive. We want to do it on offense and defense and special teams. Just go after them. I think that's what the people all over the country related to when they saw us beat Washington in the NFC semifinal playoff game in 1984. "Hey, these guys are like thugs. They don't care. They just keep pounding."

Everything we do is dedicated to Mr. Halas. Who else am I going to dedicate it to? It's funny. When I came back, there was none of that prodigal son stuff. There was no animosity. It's always amazing what you're remembered for. Are you remembered for playing hard and playing well and doing all you could for the Bears? Or are you remembered for saying Halas threw nickels around like they were manhole covers?

It was the first night after the Dallas-San Francisco playoff game in the 1981 season that Halas called me. He said, "Kid, this is George Halas." I said, "Yeah, how're you doing?" He said, "I want you to get on an airplane and fly to O'Hare. Don't tell anybody. Take a taxi and come to my place at 5555 N. Sheridan."

I didn't tell anybody, but people knew. It was the only call I got from him. He had made up his mind. It was cut and dried. He had the contracts right there. When we sat down, he said, "Tell me what your philosophy is." I said, "My philosophy is the same as yours. To win." We talked a little about a multiple offense and a little about the passing game. I told him

basically my philosophy was the same as the Cowboys. That's
where I learned. We didn't talk very long. He said, "I want you
to coach the Bears." He made me an offer of a two-year contract. I told him I couldn't come unless I had three years. He
didn't mind. If I would have said five years, I probably could
have gotten it. But I had negotiated with him so much I was
probably scared. I got paid $100,000 a year.

I've said some corny things about being a Bear. I said the
first time I put that jersey on it made me feel real good.
Brought tears to my eyes. And the last time I took it off I felt
the same way. It was that important to play for the Bears. As a
matter of fact, I wanted to finish with the Bears. I talked to
Mr. Halas after I'd played one or two years with Dallas and he
very honestly said I would have to initiate the deal. He told me,
"Try to become a free agent and we could work something
out." It never worked out. I wanted to finish my career in Chicago. Ironically, I probably am going to finish my career in
Chicago one way or another.

I'm in the process of paying dues. I think a lot of that has
been done, but I still have a few more to pay. I would like to see
the Bears the dominant team in the 80s, or at least 1986 and
1987. My contract is up after 1987 and it depends on what I
want to do. If I don't want to coach anymore, I'll say that. My
ego is not such that I have to coach. I never yet said to myself
that I want to be the winningest coach or have the best winning
percentage. All I've said is I have to pay some dues. When my
contract is up, I'll analyze what I want to do with my life. If I
think there's another challenge out there, then I might seek it.
If Dallas ever wanted to make a change, and they wanted to
consider me, that would be something to think about.

There was a time when I would have said no to everything
because it was the Bears. I say this with no dislike toward anybody. I know what it takes to be a success in life and if I'm going to be put into a confined area to operate out of, I'll go

somewhere else where I don't have to be told from a book what has to be done to make it successful. I don't think there should be any other priority except winning. I think you can win and make money, you can win and make friends, and you can win and have fun if you do it the right way. If you want to make excuses for this and that, you can. I am a Bear. That will never change. But I'm a Halas Bear. Maybe that's a dead breed now, I don't know.

II

The Super Bowl

"Okay, we've got two minutes. You did all the talking last night. The only thing that I want to say is you made your feelings clear on what has to happen. Everybody said it...Gary, Walter, Dan, Jim, Mike. You know what it is going to take. It is going to take your best effort on every play. Dedicate ourselves to that and we should have no problems. Go out and play Bear football, smart and aggressive. If something bad happens, don't worry. Why? Because we're in this together as a football team and we are going to play it for each other and we're going to win this game for 49, 50 or whatever number we have in this room. We are going to win it for each other. We are going to play it for each other and we're going to pick

*each other up. That's what it's all about. This is out of
love for each other. This is your game. Any other intentions won't be accepted. But you are going to win this
game for each other. So let's go out there and play our
kind of football. Let's have the Lord's prayer. Heavenly
Father, we are grateful for this opportunity and we thank
you for the talents you have given us, the chance to prove
that we are the very best. Father, we ask that you give us
the courage and the commitment to use the talents to the
best of our ability so that we may give the glory back to
you. Father, we ask that you may protect all the players in
the game so that they may play the game free from injury.
We pray as always in the name of Jesus Christ your son
our Lord. Amen. Let's go."*

—Mike Ditka's pre-game speech, Super Bowl XX

Pete Rozelle came up to me on the Superdome
field while we were warming up and said he was a Bear fan. I
said, "I don't think you're a Bear fan, but you ought to thank
us. We got the TV ratings back up." He said, "No, I've always
liked the Bears. I know I've been hard on you a little bit."

I got letters from him all year about players violating the
uniform code and hitting late, fighting in Dallas, having a
bounty on quarterbacks. They were on us for Jim McMahon's
headband and the ROOS on Walter Payton's shoes, for our
socks being too high. You really think they're picking on you.
I'm sure they did it with some other teams, but I think I said it
very clearly when I said there are fair-haired kids and there are
kids who are not so fair-haired in this league, Smiths and Grabowskis. I really wish we could be like Green Bay was in the 60s
or Pittsburgh was in the 70s; just go out and play and don't
worry about what they think about you, like the Raiders were.

If they think you're dirty, they think you're dirty.

We know we're not.

We were confident we could beat the Patriots. Some people wanted a rematch with the Dolphins. I didn't care who we played. I always thought the best matchup would have been the Raiders and Bears. It would have been just a brawl. I don't know how fancy it would have been or who would have scored what, but it would have been a brawl. I think we match up pretty well, although I like us at the quarterback position a little better.

Going into the game, we said it was O.K. to win it for other reasons, but if anything I would like to see us play this one for each other. That's what really counts. I wanted them to dedicate it to their teammates. We talked about the same thing after the game. We always said the Lord's Prayer and prayer of thanksgiving. It wasn't that jubilant. It was like another day at the office.

Peggy Lee sang a great song, "Is That All There Is?" And it really felt that way. The game can never match what they build it up to be. In the players' minds, after you win the Super Bowl, it's almost like a letdown because you've worked so hard for so long to do it and then you say, "I'm glad this thing is over, finally."

I think we were ready to play the week before. We had put in our game plan during the three days we spent in Champaign practicing under the bubble at the University of Illinois. The Patriots were talking about how they were a road team because they had to win three games on the road as the wildcard team. Heck, we were a road team, too. We had to practice in Suwanee, Georgia, and in Champaign.

The week of the game we had a lot of players who said too much. I think that's a sign of immaturity. I always like to be a guy who says, "Let's go do it. If we can, fine; if we can't, we'll just have to find another day to do it." But we had some people talk. But they also had some guys who talked.

The great thing about the year that was so exciting to me is as well as we played, we were completely underrated on offense. We were as good as anybody in football with our people healthy. I really believe that. We had a good line and great running backs. We were on the verge of having two great receivers and I think our quarterback is a winner, period. You can say that means he's good, great, or mediocre, I don't care. I just think he's a winner. I'd rather have Jim McMahon than the guy with the rifle arm and all the other stuff.

The way people underrated our offense, especially through the playoffs, was the most enjoyable thing to me. That we played good defense was no surprise to me. Our defensive guys epitomize the philosophy of chip-on-the-shoulder football. They don't mess around. But I thought Jim should have been the most valuable player in the Super Bowl. I have no quarrel with Richard Dent or anyone on defense. Dent was great. Dan Hampton was great. He could have been MVP. But the reason the whole thing was going on was McMahon. He put himself under pressure, behind the eight-ball, and won the game. A lot of people don't like Jim, because of the way he comes off. Maybe someday he'll change a little in that respect. But that's not going to diminish what he did on the football field. I'll guarantee you his teammates don't really give a damn what people think. They love him. And I like him, too. Walter Payton fumbled on the second play and Jim said, "It was my fault. I called the wrong play." When we signal plays in from the sideline, sometimes "24" looks like "45." We ran to the wrong side. It didn't even bother me. I just felt we would hold them there, come out of it and go to work. Jim came out and said, "My fault. I misunderstood. I should have known better than that." Well, a lot of guys would have said, "I didn't get the signal." They could have said a lot of things. But he handled that very well.

He got the week started by complaining that we didn't bring the acupuncturist to New Orleans to help his sore rear end. I agreed with him. We could have avoided that whole situation. Nobody would listen to me. I tried to talk and everybody was mad and hollering. The trainer's feelings were hurt. I don't have time as the head coach to go around to everybody in the organization and tell them that this guy is going to help, is it O.K. with them? I don't know if acupuncture helps or not, I really don't. I've taken acupuncture and it helped me some. But I said I do know that mentally, we'll have a problem. Even if it doesn't help physically, we were going to hurt them mentally. You hurt seven guys mentally, you're in trouble. They thought the guy was a guru. I didn't think it would become a big deal. I thought the players would bring him down on the Q.T. and use him. Jim was the one who said, "I can't practice without the doctor," and started wearing the headband with ACUPUNCTURE on it. By gametime, the bruise was about the size of a quarter and it didn't bother him at all.

Despite the distractions, we were able to concentrate in our practices and meetings. We had good security at our hotel. The only thing that made me mad all week was Friday night we had a meeting and they started bitching about things. They didn't get enough tickets. The hotel where their families were staying wasn't as nice. There was no cable TV over there. I said, "Wait a minute. Say anything you want to say. I know what this organization has done to try to make it run smoothly." I had been to five other Super Bowls and this was the smoothest operation I had ever seen. You can never be perfect at one of those things. Jerry Vainisi, our general manager; Bill McGrane, our marketing director; Ken Valdiserri and Bryan Harlan, our media relations people; my secretary Mary Albright; Nancy Schaffner, Donna Medica, Louise Johnson and the rest of our office people busted their tails and all of a sudden the players were going to argue about a ticket. The

Raiders are the only team that ever got more tickets. Plus, the NFL picks the hotels. They also complained about not getting enough tickets for the team party after the game. They got 10. You can't give 50 to each guy. The Cowboys always gave six or eight. I said, "Hey listen, don't come." I said, "If you lose, you aren't going to want to be around anyway. You'll be too embarrassed to show up. If you win, don't come. Let somebody else take your seats." This is on Friday! That hit me wrong. Then McMahon and some others said something about maybe the club wanting the players to pay for these things. I said, "Listen, life's too short. Don't aggravate people about not getting tickets."

On Saturday night, I said, "We've got a long day tomorrow. I don't want one guy out on the football field before we go out to warm up." They got my message. I said, "The last time we did this was when you guys were running around patting those guys from Miami on the back and they kicked our butts."

You've got to build up the "us against them" thing. Nobody likes the Bears anymore. Lots of people say how they like the Bears. They don't like the Bears; they envy the Bears. The Bears have done something a lot of people haven't done. We've done something only one other team, the 49ers, has done. That's pretty substantial.

I would say the 1963 team would have put these guys to shame on Bourbon Street. Even if we would have had to be back in, we would have brought half the street with us. That was just the way we were. These guys were pretty good, though. They didn't let any moss grow under their feet, either.

We had a curfew Friday and Saturday night. I told them to use good judgement during the week. We checked them and there was no problem. We could have fined one guy for not being in his room, but he was in the hotel. It was stupid. If he can't get off the phone by 1 o'clock, what are you going to do?

These guys think we fell off a truck. What do they think we think they're doing? They're lining up some girl. We know what they're doing. I mean it's silly. What do you think he's going to do? Call his mother at 1 o'clock in the morning and say, "Hi Mom, I want to wish you a happy Super Bowl"? They give you all this stuff about calling their aunts.

The game was over fast. We knew we could beat them with play-action passes and we knew they couldn't do much against our defense. In the second game of the season, when we beat them 20-7, we moved the ball but we self-destructed. That was the difference in the Super Bowl. It was humorous to me how all week long everybody wanted to tell us how great the Patriots were at creating turnovers. They got 16 turnovers in the three previous playoff games. All of a sudden, they forgot we led the NFL in turnover ratio all season. There was no question who the better football team was. People asked, "What do you do about them stripping the football?" We didn't strip the football. We never strip the football; we flat out knocked it out of their hands. There's a little difference. We play with a little different intensity. We don't have to strip the football the way we play. Our defense goes after people to knock it out. The Patriots have to reach and grab. I'm not slighting their coaches. If you want to coach football that way, fine. We coach a different kind of football than they coach.

The most disappointing thing about the game was Payton not getting a touchdown. I don't have to apologize to anybody. If I had it to do over, no question I would have given it to him, but I think if you really analyze his production before I got here, you have to say he's gaining more yards running the ball less now than then. His average per carry has been up since we came. We led the league in rushing three years in a row. We do all the things we have to do, but we don't look to him at the goal line. That's one thing we don't do. A lot of the reason we don't is because defenses look for him. All I try to do is put plays in that I think will score. He could have scored the first touchdown, but Jim did the right thing and took it in himself on the option. We could have handed off to William Perry every time and scored. On the play Perry scored, I guess they wanted to switch backs and give it to Payton. That's when I started hollering they were in the wrong formation. They shifted and Perry took it in. I don't worry about it. After the game, I understand had I been Walter I would have been mad at me, too. That's what I said and that's how I felt. But when it's all over, said and done, nobody's going to give a darn. With all he has accomplished in life, if scoring a gimme touchdown at the end of the Super Bowl is important, then I'm lost. He might have been disappointed in the overall game, because they keyed on him a lot and put some hits on him early. On Matt Suhey's first touchdown, Walter knocked the hell out of the safety. He'll never get credit for that, but that's what he did. His blocking was outstanding. You don't like to put one above the group, whether it be a coach or a player.

Play-action passes are a big part of our offense because teams have to respect Payton. In the Super Bowl, we didn't run as well as I thought we could. We made Willie Gault a major part of the game plan. We made the tight ends important and the backs some, but basically we were going to isolate Gault. The Patriots said they were going to cover him and we were just going to see whether their left cornerback, Ronnie Lippett, could do it. Neither Lippett nor Raymond Clayborn could. We felt he could run with anybody regardless of which one covered him. We tried to put certain formations in to have Gault isolated against Lippett. All their backs and linebackers came up and played the run very well. If you give them play-action fakes to bite on, Gault can run past them.

We also set up our pass protection so we didn't have our backs blocking their outside linebackers, Andre Tippett and Don Blackmon. We would block a tight end against one linebacker and slide away from the tight end and have a tackle or guard come out on the other outside linebacker. They didn't blitz their inside linebackers much.

Willie was a major part of a lot of game plans down the stretch. He was a major part of our passing game, period. Dennis McKinnon played so well for us in playoff games against the Giants and Rams, too. But we just needed to break the defense somewhere with a long pass and Willie just responded with some big plays for us in key situations. We usually don't try to isolate one guy, but the way he was working in practice every day, Jim was getting more and more confidence in him and throwing the ball to him.

After the pregame meal, I never ate again until the next day, so when I drank some champagne, I enjoyed it to say the least. I got about three hours sleep before I went to the press conference the next day. Then we came home and went to the parade. I'm still not sure I saw what I thought I saw. I thought it was impressive coming down the Kennedy Expressway with all the people on the overpasses hanging down. I figured by the time we got downtown, there would be 15,000 or 20,000 people. But what did they say? A half million or more? It was incredible. It's a tribute to the city and the fans.

I was happy. I enjoyed it. But I was proud. Is enjoyment better than pride? I'm proud. When we went to a Red Cloud banquet the week afterwards, a girl came up wearing a pin that summed it up. She said: "I wore this pin in your honor." It said: "We Came, We Saw, We Kicked Ass."

III

Buddy Ryan

I had only one real blowup with Buddy Ryan. That was at halftime of the Miami game, our only 1985 loss. It was a big one, no question about it. I told him very simply in the locker room at halftime, "You want to go outside right now? We'll go."

The Dolphins had three receivers in the game and Buddy was telling me a linebacker was the best guy we had to cover a receiver.

"Kiss my ass. Get somebody out there that can cover him," I said.

He said, "He covers him in practice."

I said, "He doesn't do it as well as a defensive back in practice."

He had Wilber Marshall trying to cover Nat Moore. Wilber is a hell of a football player, but do you think it's fair to Wilber to make him cover Nat Moore? I said, "Come on, we have a defensive back. Match up with him and play. Match up your best with their best." That's all I wanted to do and I asked him very simply, "Why are you doing that?" We had a pretty good shouting match on the sideline right before the half. The players saw it. When we got into the locker room, I said, "We can do it any way you want to do it. We can go right out back and get it on or you can shape your ass up." Never again do I want an argument with a coach on a sideline when I ask him what he's doing with his coverage.

Recognition is hard to come by for most assistant coaches. The way some of them do it is to have the good defense or good offense or good passing game. Then the head coach offers come in. It's always a feather in a guys' cap to say it's his offense or his defense or his passing game when really it's the Bears' offense, the Bears' defense, and the Bears' passing game.

I think every assistant coach tries to make his lamp burn a little brighter whenever he can. I think I did it in Dallas, but I would hope I never put myself ahead of the Cowboys. There was probably a time when I made myself as important as the Cowboys. Maybe it was an ego carryover from being a player. I thought I was an important player, so I think I had to be an important cog in the machine as an assistant coach. Assistant coaches are valuable. You'll never win without them. But to think you're going to gain great notoriety as an assistant, you're foolish. Buddy got as much recognition as any other assistant coach in the league.

When I came here, everybody wanted to know what offense I was going to run. They wanted to know if we were going to run the Cowboys' offense. Virginia McCaskey once told me, "I'm getting so tired of hearing this. Let's run the Bears' offense."

I said, "I never had any other concept but that."

For a long time, Mr. Halas kind of wanted a division between the offense and defense. He wanted the defense to be the bad guys, the chip-on-the-shoulder guys. They say when Halas would walk into a defensive meeting, the defensive coach, Clark Shaughnessy, would quit talking. I swear nobody knew the defenses except Clark and Bill George anyway.

I never totally understood that way of thinking, but I could see a shield existed. I don't think you can do that today. I think the defense has to have its individual pride, but you better have an offense to complement it so both sides can respect what the other is doing. Halas used to pit coaches against coaches to keep everyone in balance. He never wanted one guy to get real powerful. I don't know if you can do that today, but it's not a bad idea.

When I was hired, Mr. Halas already had retained Buddy as the defensive coordinator from Neill Armstrong's staff and also kept defensive backfield coach Jim LaRue and defensive line coach Dale Haupt. That didn't bother me one bit. I felt I could get along with anybody as long as people knew I was the boss. Ultimately, the responsibility was going to come back to me if it wasn't done properly. That's what I said to all the coaches. After the Super Bowl, I congratulated all the coaches for the job they did and the contributions to the season. Somebody said I kissed Buddy during the plane ride home. I probably did. To be honest, I never disliked anybody. If I don't like them, I don't go around them. That was not the case with Buddy. I really respected what he did in a lot of areas. Yet I don't know that he ever respected that I was the head coach. That's the only thing that bothered me. I think there was a little resentment there. I liked him; I didn't dislike him. I liked his wife, Joanie. I think there's resentment sometimes when somebody comes into an organization like I did and someone else maybe feels he should have had the job instead.

If Buddy hadn't gotten the job in Philadelphia, he would have been back here. I wouldn't have had anything to say about it. He had two years to go on his contract, just like me. I'm sure when I first came if I had wanted to fight for it with Mr. Halas, I could have made a change. I probably could have made a change after 1983, the year Halas died and Michael McCaskey took over. I felt it was a mistake after the 1984 season to go out and give him a three-year contract, but that's the owner's prerogative. I thought he was going to get the head coaching job in Indianapolis for 1985 anyway.

I lived with it very well, but I don't have to live with it any more. We don't need it, because we had a problem and that problem was one of statistics. The defense was always climbing the ladder because of statistics. I don't look at statistics. Do you win or do you lose? All we want to do is win football games and we'll let everybody take the bow. I lived with Ryan because there is no way I'll ever be stupid enough to stand up in a boat when it's going and start rocking it. Leave well enough alone and let's go.

The thing that bothered me when Buddy was carried off the field after the Super Bowl is I didn't see anybody pick up Dale Haupt after we led the league in sacks. I didn't see anybody pick up Jim LaRue when we led the league in interceptions. I get a little false feeling about all that stuff. I wish I wouldn't have been picked up at all.

The thing that Buddy did so well was get his people to believe in him and believe in the system. He relates to them. He gets it done his way. His way isn't my way. His way probably couldn't work for Landry. But his way works for him. That's important. If I have a foreman who is running a certain part of my plant and maybe I might not agree with him but his productivity is tremendous, I'd be a fool to say anything. That's what counts. Are you productive? Do you get results from your people? He did. He knew how to push those guys' butts. He knew how to push them and turn them on.

But they got to a point where they thought they could do it only one way. I don't agree with that. I think when you have good athletes, when they understand defense, they can play any number of defenses and play them effectively. You can get into a rut and say, "We can't play zone." That's bullshit. Anybody can play zone if you teach and understand zone. Everything is teachable. The thing we should never fool ourselves about is personnel. If we have good personnel, play it. If you want to talk about what's important in a coach, you better learn how to evaluate your personnel and get your best people on the field. We had a hard time getting our best people on the field. The one thing in coaching you can't do is have favorites. You're going to have some, but you can't let that override good judgement. You can't keep a guy with athletic ability off the field just because another guy knows his assignments better. In the long run, that's not going to hold up. If the assignments become a problem, then you make the system simpler so you can use a guy's athletic talent. That's the main problem I had with Buddy. The first couple years, we had a lot of people on the defense that time had taken its toll on. It was time to make some changes, period. And we made some changes and they were for the best. That's evident because the defense became No. 1 for the first time in 1984.

Don't tell me the defense was doing anything different four years ago from what they did the last two years. They did the same thing, but they did it with better people. The result comes from the players in the system, not necessarily the system. The system was here for eight years and hadn't won except for the last couple years. It started winning when Mike Richardson came in and played cornerback. It started winning when I said Mike Singletary wasn't coming off the field, that he was going to play in nickel situations. Players forget that. They think Buddy put them in.

The only reason I say it now is Buddy takes credit for doing it, which is fine if that's what he wants. But what I'm worried about is why the other guys never got to take any bows. I watch every day in practice. Who taught Richard Dent how to rush the passer? Who taught William Perry how to rush the passer? Who taught Henry Waechter how to rush the passer? Ask them and they'll tell you it was Dale Haupt. I don't want to hear all the bullshit. All I want to see is everybody taking a bow. Vince Tobin is our new defensive coordinator. His defenses were first or second everywhere he's been. Ever see Vince Tobin take a bow? Have you seen Dick Stanfel breaking his ass to take a bow? We led the league in rushing three years in a row. Did Dick Stanfel break his ass to take a bow for developing a bunch of young linemen? Mark Bortz played on defense. Tom Thayer played in the USFL. Kurt Becker wasn't supposed to be able to play. Jay Hilgenberg was a free agent. For a while, everybody thought Keith Van Horne was a wasted draft pick. You never see Dick break his ass taking a bow.

There's an old coaching philosophy to beat 'em down, beat 'em down, beat 'em down. When you get them to pulp, then you bring them up. Buddy tried to do it with Singletary. He tried to do it with Otis Wilson. He tried to do it with Marshall a year ago. That will never be done again. That way of coaching is finished with the Bears. That last four years we drafted kids high after saying we needed help at certain positions. There's an old adage that if you draft a quarterback, he's got to sit on the bench for five years. Bullshit. That's ridiculous. Draft a quarterback and if he's got talent, teach him to play now. You draft a linebacker, teach him what he has to know to play now.

I hear players say that Buddy is a father and friend. I want my coaches to be coaches and teachers. I don't particularly want them to be a father. If a player's relationship with his coach is better than his relationship with his father, he didn't have a very darn good relationship with his father. To me, a coach is a teacher and friend and somebody you can come to when you've got a problem and you can sit down and work with him. Maybe to a degree, a coach can be a father away from home. But I don't believe that was the relationship at all between Ryan and his players. I'm still not sure I understand it, but maybe that was the only way a player thought he could get on the field. Ron Rivera could have played here for 30 years and he would have never been on the field. I bet you he gets on the field in 1986. I bet he challenges people who were all-pro in 1985. Jim Morrissey never took one snap on defense in the whole season in practice, except when he ran the dummy defense against us. Incredible. Not one snap. Is that fair? I got more excited than anything when rookies like Jim Morrissey and Reggie Phillips intercepted those passes in the Super Bowl. To me, this is what the game of football is all about. This is what the Bear organization should be all about—developing young people. You don't know how good a person might be until you give him a chance to play. I don't care who you are in life, that's the most unfair thing, not getting a chance. If you're playing favorites and bullshitting a guy and telling him, "Oh, you're the greatest," that's not coaching. Coaching is not getting the best out of the best; it's not friendships or buddy-buddy or who you like or who looks good in the shower. It's getting people who don't have the true talent come up to a level that's going to help your football team. If coaching is putting it on a blackboard and telling a guy to go do it, then that would be easy. Anybody could do it. Coaching is teaching. And it's taking the time out when a guy doesn't do it right to tell him why he doesn't do it right. Show him how to do it right.

Morrissey worked his butt off, never said anything, never got a chance. That's what was happening with Perry until we took him and put him on offense. Then I said, "He's going to play on defense. He's one of the best 11."

During one game, I turned around and Buddy took Perry out. I put Perry back in. He asked what was going on. I said, "Put him back in the game where he belongs and get the other guy out of there. Leave him on the field." That was all that was said. Then he started jig-jagging him around, substituting some guys in situations for height and size. I didn't mind that. But when you really analyze it, a lot of it was to protect his earlier statements on Perry being a wasted draft choice.

We have a lot of arguments among our coaching staff. I've had arguments with Ed Hughes, the offensive coordinator, and I had arguments with Buddy. I think if you don't have those, you're really just fooling yourself. You're not really getting input from everybody. We try to get everybody involved in the game plans. You've got to use your coaches. If the head coach does all the coaching, why have assistants? If everybody agreed with me, I wouldn't need these guys. I'd just have a bunch of yes men. We argue about things and get mad and yell and holler, but when it's all said and done, we try to make the best decision for the Bears.

I used to argue in Dallas and Tom said, "I don't mind that, but when I ever feel that two coaches can't get along personally on and off the field, I'll get rid of both of them. It's very important that your argument stays within this room and it's done for the sake of the betterment of the team."

I want the assistant coaches to do their share of coaching, but I want them to do it within the framework of what we decide is best for the Bear organization. I don't think the relationships among our coaches was ever strained. I think they were as good as the relationships of coaches in Dallas or anywhere else I've been.

I feel sorry for assistant coaches in pro football because I don't think they get the recognition they deserve or the respect they deserve or the money they deserve. They put in tremendous hours and people say, "You can get an assistant coach anywhere." Well, yes, you can. There are a lot of assistant coaches and what happens is after a guy has been in the league 15 years and his salary is up high, then they hire a young guy and he'll do a good job for you at one-third or one-fourth what the other guy is making. Somewhere along the line, when these guys have contributed 20, 25, 30 years to the NFL to help make it what it is today, somebody ought to say, "Let's take care of these guys." The game can't become the game it is just because of the players. It can't become the game because of head coaches or commissioners. It becomes what it is because of all the people who make it up. The assistant coaches have a great impact on what happens and why it happens. They get very little credit. Things have gotten better. The league has tried to give more retirement and insurance benefits. It's still not as good as it should be. We have had very few changes in coaches on the Bears. I don't believe in changing. You lose a few games and what am I going to do? Fire the assistants? Yet you see this happen. It doesn't make any sense.

I'm elated Buddy had the opportunity to have a head coaching job. We'll go on and we'll do well. I was asked if I was happy he is gone. It doesn't matter. It's not that important, but yes, I'm happy we can do some things I've wanted to do. I'm going to do things my way. If the "46" defense is a good defense, we'll play it, but it will never be called the "46" in Chicago again. It will be called what Vince Tobin wants to call it. I think if you're a leader, you lead. If they are followers, they will follow. If I'm a good leader, then I'll lead the way I think I should. The guys who follow, I guarantee we'll go back to the Super Bowl. Some players have said we won't be as good without Buddy. If they feel his system is the only way they can play football and he's the only guy who can coach them, there probably will be a home for them in Philadelphia.

I would just like to know where all this stuff was four years ago or three years ago or early in 1985 when we came from behind five times in the first seven games. It was a team effort, not a defense that won, or an offense, or a kicking game. I want everybody to take a bow.

I don't hold any animosity, but when you read things about him saying he saved my job, you wonder. My wife asked me what it meant when she saw a quote: "We saved the glass-blowers' job." I don't even know what the statement means. But a man should have enough courage to say it to my face. If he had, very simply, I would have whipped his ass. I'm saying this now, because these are some things that have built up in me.

If he saved my job, I'm glad he did. I appreciate it.

GROWING UP

IV

I Hate to Lose

When I was a kid playing Little League base-ball, boy I hated to lose. I cried. It just hurt my feelings to lose. I don't like to lose. I'm not proud of that, but I just don't like to lose. I don't know how it came up. Once I was catching in a game and my younger brother Ashton was pitching. He threw a few balls, so I went out to the mound and changed positions. Then the shortstop made an error and I changed with him. The amazing thing is we had a manager and he never said anything. He just let me do it. He must have figured, "What the hell is going on?" I must have played every position. Another time, I chased Ashton home and threw a baseball at him. Not after the game, during it. That's where I was bad. It didn't matter what else was going on, I'd just jump up and do something crazy. As a kid, I was just too intent on winning.

Our whole society is built that way. I really believe this: if you accept defeat, then you're going to be defeated a hell of a lot more than you're going to win. You can be gracious in defeat, but boy I'll tell you what, you can be gracious on the outside, but you better be doing flipflops inside. If you're not churning and turning, you're going to go out and get your ass whipped next time out, that's all there is to it. You'll start accepting it. I'm not sure that isn't what happened with the Bears for a while. They didn't like losing, but it seemed to be a way of life, so they accepted it. You find ways to blow games. You find a way to blow a last-minute game in Minnesota just because those guys have purple uniforms on. That's bull, I don't believe in that.

The first game I played for the Bears was against Minnesota. It was the first game in the history of the Vikings' franchise. We got murdered. They beat our butts. It was not a fluke. During the game, the offense came off and I said something to Ted Karras, one of our guards. I told him, "Get the lead out of your ass and play harder." He took a swing at me. I was just a rookie playing my first game. I wasn't supposed to say anything, but that never stopped me from saying things anyway.

Sure, I take it too seriously. Always did. Every time you went up to bat, you weren't going to get a hit or hit a home run. Every time you went to the foul line, you couldn't make the shot. Same in football. You miss some tackles, drop some passes, blow some assignments. But I took it very seriously. I put too much pressure on myself. It was wrong, because after all, it's only a game. And I was only a kid. Yet by doing that, it made me work at it more, made me practice harder, made me become better. I don't know if that's right or wrong and I don't know how to explain that to a young person. But I just know one thing: You get out of life what you put into it. If you settle for mediocrity, you'll be mediocre. That's a fact of life. You'll pattern your whole practice schedule or whatever you do to be that way.

Somebody came up to Mozart and said, "I would give my life to play as well as you do." And he said, "I did."

Somebody asked Navratilova, "How long do I have to practice to be a champion like you?" She said, "If you have to ask, you'll never know."

Those are points in life that I really believe. When I set some goals, it wasn't to be the most mediocre. It was always to be the best kid in the playground, the best on the block, the best on the team. I don't know if that's good or bad, yet I know if you don't motivate yourself with some goals, you're not going to be anything. I do think I was too self-goal oriented. It was not that I didn't care about the team. I did because I took losses as a team very seriously. But I think you have to be careful growing up not to set too many self-goals. You can lose a team concept. You can lose your relationship with other people because you're really trying to climb too fast.

Sometimes you can lose all perspective. You can lose your temper, too, and I had a bad one. In my fifth game with the Bears, we were playing the Colts. The Colts had a linebacker named Bill Pellington. They had played the Lions and Pellington had knocked out their tight end, Jim Gibbons. Mr. Halas sent films to the commissioner saying Pellington was playing dirty. He wanted to protect me, a young rookie, who didn't have to take this crap off Pellington because it was illegal. So all I heard all week was how tough Bill Pellington was and how he was going to knock the crap out of me. Well, I lined up on the first play from scrimmage and by God they were right. He punched me right in the mouth. I wore that little thin bar that didn't protect anything. He punched me right in the mouth and I said, "Oh boy." On the next play—I don't even know what the play was—didn't matter. I didn't even care.

I don't know if it was a pass play or a run. I just gave him a head fake, drew back, and punched him as hard as I could. Well, it kind of went on like that for a while. We had a pretty good run-to. And finally, he quit bothering me. I quit bothering him. But then a funny thing happened during the game. I was downfield 5 yards on a running play and all of a sudden this thing landed in my elbow. It was this white cloth and it had a hunk of lead in it. I said, "Oh my God, this guy is trying to blackjack me!" I ran over and started yelling at the official. I showed him this thing and I was yelling, "He's got a piece of lead in this thing and he's trying to hit me with this lead!" The official said, "Give me that damn thing. It's my flag." It was the official's flag. That's the damn truth. I was so psyched on what this guy was trying to do to me that I never even stopped to think it could be the official's flag. In those days, they were white. It was funny because the official thought I was nuts. Completely crazy.

Later my rookie year, we went to San Francisco and there was a play I remember vividly. The 49ers had a defensive back named David Baker. Tough kid. Good football player. He hit Rick Casares late after a run. It was almost like Rick was tackled, started to get up, and bam, Baker came running over and really leveled Rick. Now the play was over by then, so it was really over by the time I got to Baker. I took a run from about 10 yards and just as Baker got to his feet, I hit him. Then all hell broke loose. There were people everywhere. I don't think anybody was penalized and nobody was thrown out or fined. He just gave Rick a shot and I gave him a shot. I really think a lot of the guys respected me for doing it. I was just a rookie and I really thought the world of Rick. Of all the guys I ever played with, I don't know that anybody ever played harder than Rick did. He was kind of an inspiration to me. When I'd look at him in the huddle, if he wasn't ready to play football, then I don't know who in the hell was.

I don't think anybody could have called me a dirty football player. Ray Nitschke did once, but he was wrong. It was an exhibition game in Milwaukee and there was a sweep away from me. I was trying to come across to get in front of Nitschke to block. The back cut back and Nitschke was there and the play was over. I kind of put my hands on his back to stop. He thought I was trying to clip him from behind. I made no attempt to push him. It was just an attempt to stop and I ran over him.

That night, we all went out to a restaurant and he was there, so we had a big set-to. We didn't fight. We were going to fight, but Rick was there. He said, "Well, if you're going to fight, you'll have to fight me first." Then there was no fight. We were going to go outside. There was Nitschke, Ron Kramer, Paul Hornung, Casares, myself and maybe Bill George.

He said, "I'm going to get you." I said, "If you're going to get me, you better get me good." One thing in life you've got to remember is if you're trying to get somebody, you don't get got. But I have the utmost respect for Ray Nitschke of all the players I ever played against. In the heat of competing against each other, things like that happen. I know I hit him hard and he hit me hard and I think that's where it should be left. I don't think I ever hit him outside the rules and I don't think he ever hit me outside the rules.

I guess in those days I was certainly no bed of roses myself. I was probably as big a pain in the ass as anybody. I carried a chip around pretty good. I got mad at people and I retaliated. I did go after people, but it was always within the rules. I can go back to Joe Schmidt, the middle linebacker for the Lions. I had chances to hit him low and high and I hit him high. I had a chance to hit Nitschke high and low and I hit him low, because he called me a dirty player. He just never saw me coming. I paid my dues with him many times because he knocked my ass out three or four times after that. I never said he was dirty. I always said he was tough. I'd rather play against a guy like that than a guy who would cheap-shot you. I never cheap-shotted anyone.

I had a run-in with Don Shinnick, who was playing linebacker for Baltimore. I was downfield blocking and, yeah, I put a little more into it. He wrote me a letter. I felt bad about the letter because it said I was going to get hit with lightning. But what the hell, it's only a block, only a game.

The maddest I ever got in a game was against Detroit once against Alex Karras. The play was over. I don't know what I was doing but I remember getting off the ground and Karras was going back to the other side of the ball and he just knocked the shit out of me. For no reason. He just hit me with a forearm from behind. Almost killed me. I called him every name in the book. He was just laughing. I don't think he did it to hurt me. I think he just did it to piss me off. And it worked. And what chance did I have of ever getting even with Karras in the middle of the line? I had no chance at all. I never did get near him, plus I probably didn't want to anyway.

I take the job seriously. My last year playing with the Bears, in 1966, we were in Los Angeles playing the Rams and a kid ran out on the field. He started running around while we were in the huddle and everybody was laughing. The Rams were laughing and the police were chasing him. They couldn't catch him, so I decided I was going to knock him down when he got close to me. That's what I did. He had been drinking and was probably just having fun. But I never apologized. He had no business on the field. I wouldn't walk into somebody's office and start jumping up and down on the desk.

Fans bother me sometimes on the sidelines. You hear a lot of things. I don't say very much back. I got in an argument in Tampa with a guy who was on me. I was sweating so bad I had pits under my arms and he was getting on me about deodorant and everything else. Wasn't very nice. During our first game against Dallas in 1984, somebody said something about me still being on the Cowboys' payroll. Now that's the statement of an astute fan. I said something back. It bothered me. I realize the comments of some fans are a minority, but it still bothers me. Without the fans, you don't have a game. When you pay your money, you have a right to voice your opinion. I don't argue that. I'm just saying it bothers me. I don't say I'm right; I just defy anybody else to say it doesn't bother them. I would almost like to get the Bears to a situation where nobody could say anything bad about them. I realize that's a ridiculous, idealistic situation, but that's the way I feel.

V

Aliquippa

The name was Dyzcko. That's what it was when my grandfather came from the Ukraine. My dad, Mike, changed it to Ditka. One of my uncles changed his name to Disco. My dad's other brother was changed to Discoe. My aunt and my dad are the only people who carry the Ditka name. When they were growing up, the way kids pronounced Dyzcko, it came out either Disco or Ditka. So they just spelled it the way it sounded.

There are other Ditka's, but they're not related to us. There are Sitka's and Nitka's. I ran into a guy whose name ended in Ka who said he was Czechoslovakian. On my grandmother's side, there was some Polish, but both my grandfather and grandmother came from the Ukraine.

My mother, Charlotte, is Irish-German with some English in her. Her last name was Keller, which is my middle name.

We were a pretty close family. We did things together. I have a brother, Ashton, who is one year younger, another younger brother, David, and a younger sister, Mary Ann. I remember picnics and car rides, but I was kind of an individual. I would rather have been out playing ball with a group of 10 guys.

When I was real young, my dad was away in the Marines. I didn't really get to see him until I was 4 or 5. When he came out of the Marines, we understood the rules. What he said, he said. That was it. He didn't spare the rod. I wouldn't have it any other way now that I look back on it. As a kid growing up you don't really understand those things. I didn't understand them very well even in high school. I don't know that I was really out past 11 o'clock until I was probably a junior or senior in high school. Ever. I wasn't allowed. Most nights, we were in bed by 9:30. That's the way he was raised by his father and that's the way he raised us.

We lived in a housing project in Aliquippa, Pennsylvania. It was a government-subsidized housing project. Low-class condominiums. It was a single house in a row of six houses. They were called the Projects. It wasn't a bad life. There were so many kids around. The house was small, but in Aliquippa, it was not unusual. We weren't busting out the high-rent district. We weren't threatening Beverly Hills.

But our life was a good life because the steel industry was booming. My dad worked all the time and made good money. We always ate good and dressed good. My first couple of years at school, my mom dressed me like I was Lord Fauntleroy. It was kind of silly, but that's what I wore. My dad would get the bill and pay it off over time like everybody else in the town did. The people in the town were great. They always helped. In grade school, the kids who coached us were ex-high school players. They never made anything. They just did it because they wanted to do it to help somebody else. I'll always remember that about that community and that whole valley.

It's depressing now. Places are boarded up or closed. It's a mess. A lot of the older guys who worked in the mills were first-generation European. Now these kids are second-generation and they will never know what it was like. All they know is it's bad. I guess it's an era of America that will never come back. Everybody has moved out to the suburbs and shopping centers. The town still does well in football, though. A kid I played with, Don Yannessa, coaches the team and they have won two state championships.

It was a very ethnic area, which was also very prejudiced. Whether you were a Polack or a Hunky or a Jew or a Dago or a Wop or a Cake-eater or Colored—we didn't use the other slang word for blacks—it was prejudiced. No one got away from it. I don't think anybody ever meant anything by it, but those were the terms that were used very liberally then. Every ethnic group had a club and they sponsored sports teams. There was pride in belonging to one of those clubs.

We played sports day and night. I was a better baseball player than football player because I was small. We played everything. In the spring, it was baseball until the sun went down. Football was the same way. Our fingers would crack and break open from playing basketball on the cold and wet court with a wet basketball. It didn't matter. That's all we had, so we played.

You either did that or hung around the store and learned how to smoke cigarettes and do things you were going to get in trouble over. Once in a while, we'd go out in the woods with BB guns and shoot frogs. Most of the time we played sports.

I had a temper when I was growing up, which is kind of unusual because I don't have one now. Shows how you can grow out of things. But anyway, if I struck out and slammed the bat down or threw the bat in Little League baseball, my dad knew all about it. He expected me to abide by the rules. He wanted me to do it the right way, to conduct myself as a gentleman with respect for the name which was his name. It was very important to him. He would accept the fact I struck out three or four times if I did it like a man. If I didn't, he gave me a hard time. By a hard time, I mean he simply whipped my ass. He might not attend every game, but he'd know everything that went on in the game. He got his point across. He has never watched me play golf. I don't think he is strong enough to do that.

I had a knack for getting in trouble when I was growing up. It found me. I would do silly things, pranks at Halloween, stuff like that. I was always the guy who got caught. If I didn't get caught, somebody would say they saw me there. If they saw me there, then I got my butt whipped. I wasn't the ringleader. I was one of the guys. I wasn't a bully either. I was like any other kid growing up. I got whippings for fighting. We'd play a game to keep each other from coming up the concrete steps. Once, a kid's glasses fell off and I ended up breaking them and I got a beating I never forgot. And it was my best friend, a kid I grew up with and served on the altar with for years. Looking at it now as a father, I can understand why my dad got so mad because the things we did were so trivial and didn't mean a darn thing. Yet kids feel that it's essential that they turn somebody's garbage can over or they throw tomatoes at somebody's house. If someone did that to me, I'd chase them just like those guys chased us. That was the whole thrill, when you found somebody to chase you. That made it fun. Until you got caught.

Once I snuck some cigarettes. There was a nice little field covered with woods between the bottom of the Projects and the top of the Projects. So I was sitting up in the middle of those woods. My dad always smoked Lucky Strikes. I had never smoked a cigarette, but I took a pack of Luckies and a pack of matches. I was in third grade. I lit one, puffed on it, didn't know what I was doing. I don't know if I ever inhaled, but I do remember that I got extremely dizzy and threw the cigarette away. I wasn't in good shape to begin with and then the cigarette caught the hill on fire and burned the woods. I got out of there.

My dad came home and looked out there while we were having dinner. He said, "What happened to the woods?" My mother said, "Well, you'll have to ask your son. He burned them down." I got nailed. He had an old leather Marine belt. That was probably the hardest whipping I got.

Kids just don't understand what their parents do to help them. At the time, it sure doesn't seem they're trying to help. In high school, I tried to get the car once a week. It was tough and I know I appreciated it when I got it. But I had a great record of wrecking cars. One day I was probably in the middle of the road coming around a bend and an old couple came along on my side of the road. So I swerved, they swerved and we sideswiped. That was about 800 bucks. Another time I was going to work about 5:30 in the morning and hit somebody a minute from my house. My dad didn't trust me very much with the car and I don't blame him.

I remember I always got up early. I always thought I was missing something if I didn't get up early. When I was young I always served the first mass. I'd be out at home plate when the others would come to play. I was ready to start the game. I would be on the basketball court dribbling before the rest of them got there. I was just afraid I was going to miss something. Now, I need basically about five hours sleep and one catnap. When I wake up in the morning, I can't stay in bed.

Football was an interest as far back as I can remember. I started playing organized football in fifth grade at St. Titus parochial school. We played all the other schools in that valley. Sometimes the teams we played were eighth-graders, much bigger, and we'd have some problems.

Athletics were fun, but they were a means to an end and that was to get out of that area, or at least step up. There was nowhere you were really going to go in the community if you came from a working family unless you got a college education. And the monies weren't there to send the kids to college unless you got an athletic scholarship or a scholarship of some kind.

My dad worked in the mill. He was a burner for the Aliquippa and Southern Railroad, which serviced the Jones and Laughlin steel mill. The railroad ran inside the mill and brought the coal and coke. At that time, that was the biggest rolling mill in the world and one of the busiest. Of course, that's when steel was booming. I never worked in the mills, even in the summer. I walked through the mill once with a class in school and it was very interesting. I worked for the city, for the high school, and in the state park system. I really believe my dad wanted it that way.

I saw the way my dad and my grandfather came home from work all the time. The clothes, the dirt, the filth. My dad had burn marks on his arms. All his clothes had holes in them from the sparks. That wasn't what I wanted.

My dad played some football, sandlot football. It was a semi-pro type of ball. He got slammed into a car and broke a couple ribs and that ended his football career. My dad is very, very competitive. When he takes something on, he takes it on to get it done and get it done the best way he knows how. He has a fierce amount of pride. For guys who worked in the mill, you say, "Where the hell does the pride come from?" Regardless, the pride is there, whether they were working the mill, digging a ditch, or working the coal mines.

My dad became president of the local union and ran it for years. He was a tough bargainer. He didn't defend those guys who didn't work, though. If they didn't put in their eight hours, he didn't back them in their cry against management. But the guys who did and had legitimate gripes or injury, he backed them.

My dad told me my opportunity was going to come through sports. He said I had to get good enough grades so I could get a scholarship for sports. He always encouraged me in that way. There was a time when he said, "The mill is not for you. You don't want it."

It seemed like we went to school to finish school to get out of school to go play. School was the vehicle to let you play sports, instead of sports being a vehicle of school. Not that school wasn't important, but it wasn't as important as the sports.

As a kid growing up, even if you didn't go to the football game on Friday night, the stadium was right up on the hill and we were on the other hill and you'd see the lights and hear the crowd and the noise and you'd listen on the radio and then you always had that dream of playing once you went and saw. You wanted to play in that stadium before those people.

But it didn't come easy for me in football because I just wasn't big enough when I first started. I played halfback in grade school. The quarterback got hurt, so I played quarterback. It wasn't my favorite position. We ran all those option plays and I didn't like it after I got my ass kicked. I didn't want to get hit when I didn't have the ball anymore. I only weighed 110-115 pounds and we were playing against kids who weighed 180-185. Those guys were like giants. You can imagine what we felt like.

When I was a freshman, I had a chance to become a starter when another guy got hurt. I couldn't even make it, not that I wasn't good enough, but I was just too weak to have any endurance to last. So another kid started and became a star.

I remember leaving a game and this black kid liked to beat the hell out of me. I never forgot this because one of these guys on the freshman football team jumped in and really saved my life. I had no chance. This kid was a boxer and he would have knocked me apart. It was just something for him to do. No big deal. I just happened to be there. Instead of hitting a tree, he hit me. The guy who stepped in was really the star of the football team, Bob Rembert. Walking home, he said, "Someday you and I are going to be the stars of this team anyway." I said, "Right." He was 6-4, 195, and I was 5-7, 130.

We had a really good high school coach who was a tremendous guy, Carl Aschman. He took me to camp before my sophomore year in high school. I was just a punk, 135 pounds. One of the coaches put me at defensive back. He told me the first thing I had to do was see if it's run or pass. If it's pass, I had to drop back. If it's run, I had to come up and make the tackle. They ran a draw play and I thought it was a pass. I started dropping back and all of a sudden this big lineman came downfield and just killed me. He hit me and my helmet came off and everything. Coach came running out there and said, "God dammit. Get that kid out of here before he gets killed." So they put me on duty. I cleaned the latrines. That was my duty for the rest of camp. I ate good, but I cleaned the latrines. Never got back into another practice.

I played JV ball that year and got my butt whipped and also played on the hamburger squad against the varsity. I really was going to quit football. My mother used to come to practices. Some people said she yelled at Coach Aschman for being too hard on me, but I don't know that she ever did that because I don't know that anybody ever yelled at Coach Aschman. She might have told me they were being too hard on me, because I almost quit. I was running all those dummy plays with the varsity and getting killed. First of all, I wasn't fast enough. Then I wasn't big enough. I was saying to myself, "I'm not too smart, but I'm not this dumb that I have to do this." So I went and saw Coach Aschman.

I said, "I don't think I can play. I'm too small."

He said, "No, come on out. I remember you and I remember what happened, but I saw some improvement. Anybody can quit anything. You don't have very much longer to go. You're going to get a little bigger next year and you can play."

Coming from him, I thought maybe I'd do what he said. That summer, I did get bigger. My dad is only about 5-10. My mom's family was bigger. Her dad was about 6-4. So the height came and I did everything every other kid did. I ate wheat germ, exercised, did chinups, situps, ran cross country, and did isometrics. We didn't have the weights and things they have now. I never lifted any weights until I got in college.

As a junior, I started at linebacker at about 160-165 pounds on a team that won the Western Pennsylvania Interscholastic League championship. I played end on offense, too, except when they wanted to pass they put another kid in who could run and catch. When I was a senior, he put me at middle linebacker and switched me to fullback. He said, "Do you mind playing fullback?" I said, "No, I don't mind, but I think you could have a pretty good end and you're going to have an average fullback." He said, "I'll take the average fullback." That's where I really learned how to run with the ball. It was the best thing that ever happened to me, because I learned how to run with the ball and how to use a stiff-arm. I was up to 180-185 by then. I had caught Bob Rembert as a football player. He was still a better basketball player.

My high school coach was a tremendous influence on my life because he could have said, "Hey kid, you can't make it. You're too skinny, too small, too slow. Do something else." But he never did and I think that's important. I had a chance to do other things or play other sports, but it came back to football. There was such a great discipline in football, more so than in other sports, and that's what intrigued me. But I was trying to play the game and I wasn't big enough in the beginning. Carl Aschman encouraged me.

Anyone who saw me would say I took it pretty seriously. I missed a layup once in basketball and slammed my fist against the wall and broke my wrist. Stupid. It all went back to Little League baseball and football. I think it was just too much emphasis on wanting to excel, wanting to be the best, and wanting to win. Those things are really blown out of proportion for youngsters in our society.

I didn't blame others when I didn't do well. I blamed myself. I took everything out on myself, but that's bad in a way. That was a lot of my problem my first year coaching the Bears. You expect too much of yourself and there's only so much you can control. It's idealistic to say the coach can control everything. It's foolish. It's like saying, "Fire the manager." Why? Because some guy can't tell the difference between a ball and a strike? Or some guy can't catch a ball when a man is on first and second and they score a run and win the game?

I'm too serious about too many things, except golf. I'm REALLY serious about that. But I don't get as mad on the golf course as I used to.

My dad has a temper. My mom has one, too. I've seen enough arguments growing up that I know they both have tempers. My dad didn't like to see me have a temper, because having something doesn't make it right. It can be all right if you use it in the right way. When you're a player, it's good to have a temper because you're called a competitor. As you get older and become a coach, then you're a hothead.

I had only one idol growing up and that was Stan Musial. I was always a St. Louis Cardinal baseball fan. Musial was from Donora, Pennsylvania, and that's probably why. Plus, I still think he was the best baseball player who ever lived.

My dad took me to the Pirates' games a few times. We'd go see Milwaukee when they came in. Warren Spahn, Joe Adcock, Johnny Sain, Lew Burdette, Johnny Logan. That was a pretty big luxury.

In football, I became an Eagles' fan. Don't ask me why. I followed Pete Pihos, Steve Van Buren, Tommy Thompson, Bucko Kilroy. But I didn't see the Steelers play live until I was in college. I used to be an usher at the games. We'd make extra money selling programs. That was when you didn't get anything for going to college except an education and $14.96 a month for laundry. That's a fact.

VI

Football and Pitt

I liked school. I didn't dislike school. I didn't like math. I had a bad math background. I liked history and all those kinds of subjects. Math gave me a lot of problems. I was an above average student and math brought me back to average.

I had a couple of chances to sign a baseball contract out of high school. I had started out a catcher, then moved to shortstop and the outfield and back to catcher. Cincinnati and Milwaukee showed some interest. I had a little trouble with curve balls, but I could have played, I think. I was playing semi-pro when I was 15 years old. Semi-pro was a pretty big deal back then and I started playing with guys who had been up in the majors. When I was 15, I saw some pretty frightening curve balls. The only thing I didn't like about a baseball career was you had to go to the minors. I wanted to go to college.

I wanted to go to Notre Dame all the time I was a kid. I always listened to Notre Dame on the radio and being a Catholic, that was a great thing. I heard from Notre Dame, too. I heard from them first and I never heard from them again. The first letter I got was from Jim Finks. He was an assistant coach under Terry Brennan, but he left Notre Dame and went to Canada. The next Notre Dame letter I got was from Bernie Crimmins. I went to visit, but it was summer and no one was there. I had already nailed it down to either Pitt or Penn State.

The guy who recruited me at Penn State was Joe Paterno, who was Rip Engle's top assistant. The guy at Pitt was Jack Wiley, who was John Michelolsen's assistant. To this day, my parents wish I had gone to Penn State. They don't regret I went to Pitt, but they were really impressed with the Penn State people and program. Joe Paterno impressed them. But I wanted to be a dentist and that entered into my decision. Pro ball was never a consideration at that time. Dentistry was the consideration. I remember talking to an athlete at Penn State who was an All-American in baseball. He said if I wanted to be a dentist, I should go to Pitt, because it was easier to get into dental school there.

My high school coach said to make sure I got everything out of college education I could. It seemed like every football player for a long time went to school to be a doctor or a dentist. A couple of dentists in Aliquippa had gone through Pitt as athletes. I spoke to them and it was something that seemed like a good profession. In retrospect, probably the last thing I ever wanted to do was stand on my feet all day and work in somebody's mouth. It doesn't make any sense at all now. But growing up, people always say, "What do you want to be?" And you'd say, "A fireman." That was impressive. I'd say, "I want to be a dentist."

I took all the courses and had trouble with chemistry. Physics was all right, but the chemistry murdered me because I had a bad math background.

I played football, basketball, and baseball in high school and I played all three at Pitt. But football was the one I liked most. Football won out because of all the education possibilities. It was a chance to get a scholarship. That's the one I worked the hardest at. I liked the nature of the game and the nature of the animal playing the game. Football probably has a lot of meanings to a lot of people, but to me when you step onto the football field everybody's equal. And when you step off, everybody's not equal anymore. Somebody's won and somebody's lost. Somebody's dominated and somebody's been dominated. Somebody's taught and somebody's learned. That's what was so exciting to me—the challenge of going out and competing and going head-to-head, man-to-man. Ernie Hefferle, one of my college coaches, always said a good way to be a good college player was to make your opponent's all-opponent team every week. Concentrate on whipping him, then worry about whipping the rest of them. That's what it was that appealed to me. Besides, in other sports, you have to use your head.

At Pitt, I played end on offense, sometimes tight and sometimes split. On defense, I was in a three-point stance playing against offensive tackles. I hardly ever stood up. I liked defense better than offense. I was a better defensive player. Even in high school, I played much better defense. I enjoyed the tackling. It was a chance to be more aggressive. Offense was kind of a controlled thing. Defense provided the aggressiveness, the combat I liked. Blocking, I didn't mind. I didn't mind catching the ball and all those things. That was fun, but on defense you could really challenge people. When teams ran the option play, it was fun because it didn't matter where the ball went. They would only run it my way one or two times and that was it. They never came back, because I just hit the quarterback as hard as I could. I didn't care where the ball was. My role was to hit the quarterback. Then they'd go the other way and I got to chase them. It made my job easy. That's the truth. It's more fun to be the hitter than the hittee. I liked to catch the ball and run with it. That's when I really started enjoying offense, when I found out after you caught it you could run with it. You could be aggressive in that area by defying people to tackle you. That became fun, too, but I didn't get to catch the ball a whole lot in college. Defense won out.

College was a time of really proving myself. I had a lot to prove. I wasn't as big a name as some of the other guys at Pitt. I wasn't as impressive early as some of the others. I think that's where I understood the harder you work the more you get out of life. I worked my tail off and I became a pretty good football player, not because I was faster or could catch the ball better, but I taught myself to do a lot of things that other guys didn't. I taught myself to punt the football and I became a pretty good punter.

Everything was competitive. My whole life was based on beating the other guy, being better, being equal to, showing that I could be as good as anybody else. That's the way I grew up. I don't know if that's good or bad.

I got knocked off my pegs a few times in college when I was supposed to be a good player. My junior year, we played down at West Virginia and I was all-preseason this and all-that. If a guy could get his ass beat any worse than I did that game it would be hard to believe. They made it a point to run the football at me and they had a fullback who knocked my ass upside down, inside out and all around. When he didn't knock me down, someone else did from somewhere else. Finally, Coach Michelolsen took me out of the game. Basically, I had quit playing the defense and started playing my own freelance

game and it really hurt our team and they upset us. Michelolsen took me down a couple of pegs, which was great. He let
me have it pretty good in front of the team. The next week, we
played TCU. We lost that one, too, but the caliber of my play
improved tremendously because I realized I couldn't do it by
myself. I was trying to be too much of an individual.

The next year, we beat West Virginia 42-0. The guy I was
out to get was the fullback who had kicked my butt. He was
still there. They opened the game coming at me and I stopped
it for no gain. They came back a couple plays later and I
played just so much better. I caught a touchdown pass, the
longest one I caught in college, about 48 yards.

In my junior and senior years, I played about 55 minutes a
game. The coaches used to say I couldn't play more than four
minutes at a time because I'd get so exhausted. They were
probably right in the beginning. I mean I was really hyper. I'd
go out and I'd just go full tilt. I'd get so damn tired, I'd have to
rest a play. It wasn't because I wasn't in shape. It was because I
was hyper.

Hefferle used to say I pounded guys something awful,
even my own teammates in practice. He said if we didn't watch
out, I'd kill everybody off. But Ernie's the one who created
most of that. Ernie's the one who said, "Beat the shit out of
the guy. Line up over the guy and knock his head off. Make his
all-opponent team." That's all he ever told me. And he was a
good coach. He taught us how to play the game. He used to
love it when we scrimmaged. He'd say, "They're going to run
that option and you hit that quarterback. I don't care where
the ball goes. Hit that quarterback the first time and they'll
never run that option again."

He wasn't far from right. We played Miami in 1960, the
year they had the World Series in Pittsburgh. We had to play at
10 o'clock in the morning. Miami had an option quarterback

and they were really doing well. The first time they came my way, I hit him and the ball went one way and he went the other way and I went another way. We recovered the ball. About the second quarter, he came my way again and I hit him again. When I got up, I said, "I'm going to hit you that hard, I don't care if you have the ball or not. You might as well start going the other way." I don't think he ever came my way again. Ernie was laughing.

When I was a sophomore, I had played a lot in the first six games, but I'd been a backup. Then Notre Dame came into town. They had their alumni get-together on a Friday night and Terry Brennan said Pitt had an end who would be starting if he had gone to Notre Dame. Lo and behold, Saturday I started. Michelolsen started me for the first time ever. He must have read the paper. I really did play a good game. I punted well, caught a couple passes, played good defense. The game sort of sparked my career. We ended up beating them 29-26 in the last minute with an option play. They had Monte Stickles and Bob Wetoska on that team and Bobby Williams was their quarterback.

Our teams were good, but never great. My senior year, we were 4-3-3. We had three 7-7 ties. I was a captain and I was pretty outspoken. There was an incident during the Michigan State game I remember. Right before the half, a guy caught a long pass and ran for a touchdown. We had a defensive back who dropped an interception. We were coming into the locker room and he said, "Well, we're only down 7-0. It's only half-time." I said, "Seven-nothing? That's bullshit. It doesn't matter what we're down. You had a chance to make a play and you didn't make it."

It was probably wrong to say it, but that's what I confronted him with. He was a good friend of mine, a Christian kid from Mt. Lebanon. In fact, he became a minister. He took what I said as a big offense, I'm sure. He didn't talk to me for about a day. I went down and apologized to him the next week in the dormitory. I'm sure I hurt his feelings and I'm not saying I was right. But at the time, I thought I was. We tied Michigan State, TCU, and Army that year, lost to UCLA 8-7, lost to Oklahoma 15-14, and got beat by Penn State 14-3. We were 17 points from being undefeated. But it's not important? What's important is that we only won four games.

I never was a bully. I've challenged a few people I thought were giving less than total effort. I'm sure that didn't make them too happy. But I was the captain of the team and that was my right to say, "Hey, let's either do it or don't do it. If you don't, we'll get somebody else out there."

There's a story about me punching out two guards in the huddle, Ralph Conrad and John Draksler. I remember talking to them, but I don't think I ever punched them. They were too big. The stories about me at Pitt get better every year. I keep reading about all these bars I was in. I was hardly in any bars until my senior year. We cut a wide swath then, though.

I was outspoken sometimes. Before we played Syracuse when I was a junior, I said, "If we play like we practice, we're going to get beat 50 to nothing." We got beat 35-0 and the coaches got mad at me for saying it. After it was over, Michelolsen called me in. I said, "Hey, you gotta admit I wasn't far wrong." He said, "You can't say those things." I said, "Coach, you saw the practices last week. They were horseshit." That didn't endear me too much to him, I'm sure.

I was a nice guy in college. One time, we were playing TCU at TCU and a big fight broke out. I mean a really big one. People were coming out of the bleachers and everything. I was really trying to be a good guy. I was the captain. Plus my roommate was the guy who started the fight. I was walking up the field and I hadn't gone 10 yards when I got decked so hard from behind it was incredible. It was a TCU player named Arvie Martin. I got up and it was a matter of wondering what I was going to accomplish. I thought, "Who are you going to hurt anyway?" He called me a sissy. I never did fight in the game and I guess that's why he made the comment.

Those ties made it a funny year. In the TCU game, I caught a pass but the official said it hit the ground. The ball was deflected and I turned around and dove and caught the ball before it hit the ground. I ranted and raved about it. Michelolsen said, "Son, you didn't catch the ball. We could see it from the sidelines." I said, "Coach, I caught the ball." They looked at the film and I caught the ball. It was fluky, but I caught it. It was a big play because we could have kicked a field goal and won the game.

In the Army game, another 7-7 tie, there was a pass thrown to me and Glenn Adams intercepted. I got knocked down and he made a long run, but he had to reverse his field and I took off and finally caught him. I was really out of it. I mean I was dead and I had to get oxygen after the game. There is a story that one of the Army players came up to me and said, "You're the greatest football player I've ever seen." It was probably my dad. I don't really remember what anybody said to me.

Those service teams were really tough back then. I'd go up against guys on other teams that weighed 245 or 250 and I'd go up against those Army tackles who weighed 220 or 225 and they were twice as strong. I played against the Naval Academy when I was a freshman. Played against Joe Bellino. He rushed for 240 yards. We outweighed them 50 pounds a guy.

In four years at Pitt, I never played with a black kid on the football team. I played with them my whole life and they were the best on the baseball, basketball, and football teams. We never had any problem. But at Pitt, we had only one black kid walk on the team and he never played. Even on the basketball team, there were only one or two black kids. We weren't a very good team, needless to say.

I played basketball and baseball in college. I caught in
baseball and played the outfield some. The best ball I ever hit
was up at Bucknell. My brother Ashton was playing for Bucknell. It was maybe the best ball I ever hit in my life. In basketball, in the vernacular of that day, I was called a hatchetman. I
thought I could play, but if I could make the team, you know
Pitt basketball wasn't outstanding. I played against Jerry West
at West Virginia. When I see him I always remind him I was·
the guy who guarded him for six points and three fouls in a
period of 51 seconds. He had six points and I had three fouls in
less than a minute. He tells me, "I thought you were going to
kill me." I tell him, "I was trying, but I couldn't get close
enough."

I played against Tony Jackson at St. John's and Tom
Sanders at NYU, but my fondest memory was a Kentucky
game in Lexington. We had a kid on our team from Kentucky
who fouled out about five minutes into the game. I went in and
was playing guard. They were running kind of an outside
weave and they were picking me. The guard was getting some
outside shots. I was guarding him and being a nice guy going
around this pick all the time. So finally, they set a pick right in
front of their bench. I weighed about 217 then and I was in
good shape. I could run. I hit the guy as hard as I could.
Knocked him into about the third row. Adolph Rupp came after me, swearing at me, calling me nothing but a hatchetman. I
gave him a couple of choice words back. It was reported that I
said, "You should know, you got a whole team of hatchet-
men." But I probably said something a little cruder than that. I
think I told him to shut up and sit down, you old goat. Of
course, it was sacrilegious down there to say anything to Coach
Rupp. Of course, me being not too smart and not a basketball
player, it didn't matter. I just didn't understand why they were
allowed to run moving picks. I wasn't going to allow it to happen. It was the best game I ever played. I scored 17 points. At

least I thought I scored 17 points. We got beat, but there were 17,000 people in that arena and they stood up en masse and booed me anytime I did anything. It was really fun.

John Erickson, who used to coach at Wisconsin, said he used to watch me and said it was amazing. He said, "You were like a bowling ball. You'd just go out and knock people down."

I didn't graduate from college. I got a good education, but I didn't graduate. My whole thing was based on being a dentist. I had all the other credits, but I had to make up a small number of hours—all in chemistry. I have a love of chemistry that's unbelievable. I could never force myself to go back and face the chemistry courses.

I think a kid getting a scholarship to play sports in college is signing a contract. The college has obligated itself to give him an education for playing sports. If the guy gets hurt, he should still finish that education. The athlete also should finish the four years he owes the college. I don't believe in kids jumping school early. I don't think you can go to school until you get a better deal. There is so much pressure to win in college nowadays that they go outside the rules. Pitt was legitimate and Penn State was legitimate and Notre Dame was legitimate, but some of the schools that recruited me weren't legitimate. In certain schools, you were in the $50 a month category or the $100 a month category or $200 a month category. I never got to the $100 or $200 category, but I got to a couple that offered me $50 a month.

They talk about people above the coaches who condone the cheating. I don't know the answer. I just know no matter what set of rules you set down in any form of society, people break them. The punishment for murder is a lot worse than it is for cheating, but people still kill people. It's good to say you have an ethics committee and all this, but I think that when the game becomes more important than the outcome of the game, then you won't have the cheating. But the outcome of the game means big money. I know there are a lot of college coaches who would never do anything illegal. I know there's probably a few who would do something illegal. I don't know where I'd fall because I've never been put in that situation.

TURNING PRO

VII

I Was a Bear

Pro football became a consideration after my junior year at Pitt. I made most of the preseason All-American teams, so it was something I started thinking about. I wasn't thinking, "Hey, this would be a good way to make a living." I was thinking, "I wonder if I'm good enough to play against those guys up there." That was the whole thing. You wondered. Everything was like a stage. I never came to the Bears with the idea I was going to be anything. I just wondered what it was going to be like, how I would play against those guys.

The only thing I knew about the Bears was they were tough guys. I knew about Bill George because he was from Pennsylvania. I knew about Rick Casares and Harlon Hill.

Monsters of the Midway. I kind of always liked that, but I never knew that much about them.

My roommate at Pitt was from Baltimore and we listened to a game in 1960 between the Bears and Colts when Lenny Moore took the ball off J.C. Caroline in the end zone and the Colts won in the last two minutes. That was the first time I ever listened to a Bears' game.

I was drafted No. 1 by the Bears and No. 1 by the Houston Oilers of the American Football League in the 1961 draft. The Oilers said they would make me an offer as soon as I got back from the Hula Bowl. First, I went to the East-West Shrine Game in San Francisco, where Joe Kuharich was one of the coaches. Fido Murphy was there, driving us crazy. He was an old scout who used to work for Halas and for Mr. Rooney with the Steelers. He was chasing me and Myron Pottios, who had been drafted by the Steelers. This was at the start of the NFL-AFL signing wars. We had to sneak out windows to get away from him.

Coming back from the Hula Bowl, I was supposed to have a flight straight to Pittsburgh out of San Francisco. When I got to San Francisco, Kuharich had changed tickets on me and I went to Chicago. In Chicago, I had to change planes and get on a plane to Pittsburgh. When I changed planes, the guy beside me was George Allen. He was Halas's assistant in charge of the draft. He introduced himself, came to the house, and started talking money. He called Mr. Halas on the phone and I talked to him. He offered me $12,000.

"Biggest contract we've ever paid since Red Grange," Halas told me, which was an out-and-out lie. He said he would give me a $6,000 bonus. I said to my dad, "What do you think?" He said, "That's a lot of money. You work a long time to get that kind of money."

I never really had a choice because I was going to play in the NFL. That was definite. I was going to find out if I could play in the best league if I was going to play. Houston had flown me up to Boston for a game between the Oilers and Patriots. When I was in New York for the *Look* All-American team, Oilers' owner Bud Adams had given me three 100-dollar bills and said, "Have a good time in New York." That was a lot of money then. When I left New York and went back to Pittsburgh, I still had those three 100-dollar bills. I gave them to my mother because that was more important than spending them.

I signed the contract with the Bears and I met with Houston the next day and never told them I'd signed. The Oilers offered me a two-year deal for $50,000 and I had signed a one-year deal for $18,000. The Oilers probably could have offered me $100,000 and I still would have gone with the Bears. I was trapped. Had to make the best of it. I liked Allen. We always got along. He was just doing what Mr. Halas wanted him to do—sign me to a low contract.

I never had an agent, never in my whole life. Why would you need an agent? Why would you need a guy like Leigh Steinberg throwing out all these statements about bidding wars, so he can bring out another great Steve Young? As good a football player as Steve Young is, he proved in the United States Football League you can't win with one person. The kid got his butt whipped. If Steve had it to do over again, he'd say, "Take these millions and get me an offensive line I can live with."

It was exciting to negotiate your own contract. You negotiated face-to-face and you got embarrassed. Halas embarrassed you. Ripped you apart. After I signed my first contract for $12,000 plus the $6000 bonus, I made rookie of the year and all-pro. I came back and he offered me $14,000.

I said, "Coach, you're making a mistake. I made $18,000 last year. You're giving me a $4,000 cut."

He said, "How do you figure you made $18,000?"

I said, "12 and 6 is 18."

"Well," he said, "The 6 was a bonus, remember? The bonus doesn't count."

We went through the whole thing, back and forth. Finally, I said, "Look, I won't sign for a penny less than $18,000."

He said, "O.K., sign right here."

He had me. Anyway, I was a Bear. I kind of belonged here.

I really wasn't a 49er. I might have been a Steeler. The Bears and Steelers were close. I wasn't an Eagle or a Packer. I was kind of like a Bear. I don't want to say I had the Bear mentality. The Bears were hitters and I liked to hit and that was it.

My first impression of Halas was tremendous respect. I was 21 when I came into the league and this guy coaching me was 66. But you didn't know that. I never thought he was 66 when I saw him as a rookie. No way. The guy was a bundle of energy. I just assumed he was in his 50s. Here they tell you in society you can't work over 65 and he won a championship when he was 68 and he should have won another when he was 70 in 1965. My first impression wasn't awe, but it was tremendous respect. I don't think the respect ever left even though we bantered and argued.

Before I joined the Bears, I was with the College All-Star team that scrimmaged them. I had been wondering how I would do against these guys. After we scrimmaged, I found out they were just people. They beat you and you beat them sometimes. I can still remember my first scrimmage against the Bears when I was with the All-Stars. The Bears had a defensive back named Pete Manning. I'm not sure whether one of the coaches told him to get after my ass because I was the Bears' first draft choice or what. I almost destroyed him. I decked him on a block downfield. Later on, I was told when they were looking at the film, Halas said, "Who the hell hit Manning?"

"That's your first draft choice," they told him.

"That's O.K. then," Halas said.

The Bears needed a tight end. They had lost Willard Dew-veall to the American Football League. They were trying to convert Harlon Hill and they had Jason Arness from Michigan State. The players helped me a lot. Guys like Bill George took time to show me the tricks of the trade. Playing tough and hard wasn't a problem, but I needed to know the skills involved.

When I came out of the All-Star game and joined the Bears' camp, we played the Eagles in an exhibition game in Hershey, Pennsylvania. I knew I could play against the pros by now. The only question I had about my talent was not whether I could hit with people. My question was speed. I had only been with the Bears four or five days. I had been sick and had lost weight. I didn't play the first quarter. Then Halas put me in and they hit me with a look-in pass and I ran 70 or 75 yards for a touchdown. The guy chasing me was Irv Cross and he didn't catch me. Then I said I knew I could play. It was my confidence builder.

Since I had been sick, I couldn't wait to get into the locker room at halftime and get something to drink. A bottle of Pepsi was setting up by the fountain and it looked like it had just been opened. So I reached up and took a swig of it. I almost died. Max Swiatek, who was Halas's sidekick for years, came running over and grabbed it out of my hand. It was the Old Man's and it was half bourbon.

We got beat in my first game by Minnesota in the Vikings' first game ever. They were a new franchise and they killed us in Minnesota. Halas was mad. He said nothing after the game. We were in the air coming back to Chicago and nothing was said almost the whole way. We were almost in Chicago and all of a sudden the loud speaker came on:

"You dirty bunch of sissies."

He didn't say sissies, but you get the idea.

There are a million stories about the Old Man and his money, but he did a lot for his players. My second year, I said,

"Coach, I need to borrow some money. I want to get into the bowling alley business." The first advice he would give everybody was to buy a house. He would say, "Don't rent. Buy a house. Get some equity." He would always ask how you were doing. He would ask about the house. He always wanted to know what you had in equity. When I asked him about the bowling alley, he asked, "Who are the people? Are they good people?" I told him one was one of his ex-ballplayers. He said he would show me how to do it. We went over to American-National Bank and borrowed $12,000 at 4 percent interest, which was prime. When we won the championship in 1963, I paid the note back. There were other times when I needed something, he gave it to me. I think when I left here I owed him money. I was probably one of 50 who owed him money that he never got back. But nobody ever tells you that side. They don't tell the stories about how many times he bailed someone out of a bad jam. I know he helped Bill George a lot, and Doug Atkins, and Harlon Hill, and Bronko Nagurski. He helped Willie Galimore's family and Brian Piccolo's family after their deaths. I think that was an element that made you closer to the club and more obligated to the club and I think that was good. It was a loyalty thing and I'm sure he wanted it that way. You wouldn't see that now. Now, you negotiate a contract and the guy says, "I want a $500,000 interest-free loan."

One of my favorite stories is about Ed O'Bradovich negotiating with him. Ed made up his mind that he had to have a certain amount of money. He said he was worth a raise of $4,000. The Old Man told him how bad he'd played and how much money the Bears were losing. Ed lowered it to $3,000. Then Halas would accuse Ed of whoring around and hanging around with the wrong crowd and not doing his calisthenics properly. Ed lowered it to $2,000. Halas would go on and get it down in Ed's mind to $1,000. By the time they were through,

Ed stood up and said, "Hey coach, let me give you a check for $500."

On the other hand, I know Joe Marconi wanted to go out making $25,000. It was after 1963 and Joe had a great year. He was the whole offense in the championship game. He wanted that $25,000. He was making $23,500 or $24,000 as it was. It was only a $1,500 or $1,000 raise, just to say he made 25 grand. They went back and forth and Halas said, "Kid, I really just couldn't do that. That base contract I think we'll just have to leave at $24,000." Joe thought, "Well, I gave it a try." Then he left and as he was leaving, Frances Osborne, Mr. Halas's secretary, called him over and handed him an envelope. In the envelope was a $1,000 check. It wasn't on the contract. Had to be his way. The last contract I played for with the Bears was for $25,000 and Halas wouldn't sign it. He made his son Mugs sign it. I told him I wasn't coming to camp unless I got $25,000.

As you got to know him and were around him, you found out he played a game with people and he knew how to play it as good as anyone. He was crafty. He had a way to maneuver and manipulate and change and end up getting it done the way he wanted it done. I guess all great people do.

We used to practice on Sunday in training camp. It was not an earth-shattering practice, but after one Saturday practice, we went out to the beer garden and came back to the meeting that night. I think Halas had a beer, too, so we were even. The guys were bitching and wondering why we had to practice on Sunday. So finally, Stan Jones was designated as the spokesman. He raised his hand.

"Coach, I'd like to ask you a question."

"O.K. What is it?" said Halas.

"Why do we practice on Sunday?"

I'll never forget this. The Old Man said, "Stan, you know why we practice on Sunday? Because we practice on Sunday."

That's exactly what he said. That was the end of it.

After the 1963 championship, we were all waiting for a gift from the Bears. We'd all heard stories about how the Packers got mink coats for the wives and color TV sets. Stan Jones had told his wife, Darlis, to call him the minute anything came in the mail. Finally, this small package arrived and Darlis called Stan home. He was working somewhere in the off-season. Stan said, "Well, you know how they say big things come in small packages." They got excited and started opening it up. It was a paperweight from the City of Chicago. It slipped out of their hands and fell through their glass coffee table. Cost them $200 to get their gift from the Bears.

Teams used to pay the officials after games. All the officials would come into Halas's office in Wrigley Field after the game and settle up. He would count out the money and put it in piles. This was when they had to travel by train and the Old Man had the train schedule.

Once, after a particularly bad day when Halas felt they hadn't done a good job, he looked at his watch and started counting the money. He knew the train was pulling out at 4:45, so he watched his watch and counted out each pile, one for each official. He counted it and recounted it, all the time looking at his watch. Just about 10 minutes before the train was supposed to leave, he scooped up all the money and said, "O.K. you sons of bitches," and he threw it all at them. All over the place. A guy told me the officials were scurrying around picking up those bills. And the Old Man wasn't laughing when he did it.

You could see the drive and motivation and enthusiasm in Halas every God darn day he was up. He was a really enthusiastic guy. He was excited about what he was doing. If I live that long, I guess I'd be darned excited about trying to coach when I'm 65, too. It's amazing when you think about it. We're all out on the farm when we're 65. This guy was in the middle of his career believing he could do anything. I believe part of it was he didn't want to turn the reins over to anybody else. I don't believe he ever saw anybody he thought was capable of taking the reins from him. He fooled around with it a few times during the war and after the war. Ralph Jones and Hunk Anderson and Luke Johnsos and Paddy Driscoll all took turns coaching, but it always came back to him. I think the thing was he was just excited about HIS Bears. HIS football team. He loved the city, but this was something he created himself. He built it, he molded it and he persevered through bad years and that's why he fought so hard for a damn buck. When you sit back in retrospect and analyze that, it was right, by God, it was right. Right now, he's doing flipflops in his grave. He can't believe what's going on right now, I know that.

VIII

Reprobates

In 1963, the Bears had a bunch of reprobates. The diversification in personalities was tremendous. Hell-raisers anonymous. Halas kept them all playing. Doug Atkins couldn't play for Paul Brown in Cleveland, but he played in Chicago and went to the Hall of Fame. His personality rubbed Paul wrong and probably rubbed Halas wrong, too. But Halas knew how valuable he was to the Bears. That's so important.

Of all the guys I played with, the guy I'd most like to see play today is Doug in his prime. Against these guys today, I think you would really understand how good a football player he was. He had every quality. He had strength, he had size, quickness, speed, jumping ability—everything you looked for. With today's training procedures—and I'm not saying Doug would have followed them like these kids do now—I would have liked to have seen him. He was before his time. I really think he'd make people like Mark Gastineau and Lyle Alzado just another player. That's just the way I feel. In those days, athletes didn't take care of themselves as well as they do now. If he would have taken care of himself, I don't know how you would have stopped him.

The best story about Doug is the night we all came in from a night out in Rensselaer, Indiana, at training camp. Doug and some guys were down in Rich Kreitling's room throwing darts. We came in after being out at the local establishment. We had had a few beers. Everybody was crowded around and got into this dart thing. The dart board was setting up on a desk by the window. O'Bradovich came in and said, "Hi, big guy, whaddaya doing?" Then O.B. starting fooling around.

Doug said, "We're playing darts. Behave."

O.B. said, "Hey, let me show you how to throw those darts."

O.B. grabbed some darts and started throwing them. He was missing and fooling around.

Doug said, "Don't do that. We're throwing darts."

Doug grabbed the darts back. Ed grabbed one and threw it. Then he grabbed another one and threw it.

Doug said, "Cut it out."

Finally, Ed grabbed one and threw it. It missed the board, broke the window, and went out the window.

Doug grabbed Ed. Ed weighed 250 pounds. Doug picked him up over his head and threw him on the floor. The floor was made out of tile. That was it. Like a little dog, Ed got up, crawled away, and everybody disappeared. Nobody said anything. I was standing in the doorway and I went right down the hallway and went to my room. Not a word was said. It was like "Oh-oh. The Big Guy has spoken."

Once, Doug woke Mr. Halas up and took a chair and put it up against the door and sat in it. Wouldn't let Mr. Halas out and he wouldn't leave. He said, "Now we're going to talk, you old S.O.B." They talked. I guess he kept him up until 3 or 4 in the morning. Everything he didn't like about him, he told him.

I think Mr. Halas liked and appreciated Doug Atkins more than all those other guys. You know why? Because he always knew where he stood with Doug. He would call Doug on the phone and call him a no-good S.O.B. and Doug would call him one back. He always knew where he was. I think he always respected Doug more than the other guys for that reason. And Halas liked a good argument. He liked a confrontation. Plus, he knew he could win with Doug playing for him. Halas always put the best players on the field. You can't be narrow-minded as a coach.

After Doug left the Bears and went to the Saints, there was a story about a rookie who was playing the radio. Doug went upstairs and said, "Hey, I'm an old man. I need my rest." He went back down and went to sleep. About 2 in the morning, the radio woke him up again. Doug walked back upstairs. Pow! Pow! Pow! He shot the radio with a gun. Turned around and walked out.

Rick Casares used to tell the story about going to Knoxville, where Doug went to college at Tennessee. Rick went into a bar, a college hang-out, and got a beer. After a while, he walked over to the bartender and said, "Have you seen Doug Atkins?" The bartender ducked and said, "Where's he at? Where's he at?" Scared the hell out of him.

Rick said the guy was reaching under the bar for a club or something. I guess Doug had quite a reputation.

Doug and Fred Williams got into a martini-drinking contest once. Fred said they both drank 21 martinis but Doug won the contest because he carried Fred home. I don't know that I counted how many they had, but I know Doug used to drink martinis out of a water glass. I know he used to drink six or seven of them that way. One Pro Bowl in Los Angeles, we went out to Santa Anita to the race track. It was a party at the Pro Bowl. No one took it seriously. That's when Doug had his so-called heart attack. He thought he was dying. He passed out, and then he swore off drinking. A doctor told him he had to slow it down, so they put him on a diet where he could only have two or three drinks a day. So Doug used to start drinking late at night. He would have his three drinks for that day and then drink three more for the next day right after them.

He was a classic. That era is gone. Those were wonderful people.

Rick Casares was like Dennis the Menace. He would get in more trouble than anyone. Even if he didn't do anything, it would come up to Rick. He did a lot of things, too. And lie with a straight face. He was the best.

We would be going to Minnesota. Guys would get on the airplane with a garment bag. The Old Man would be right in front. If he saw a big garment bag, he would say, "You dirty whore. This is not a two-suit trip." It was a big joke after that. We always wondered whether we were going on a two-suit or a one-suit trip. Rick would always say, "Well coach, I have to go out to dinner with my friends, then I have to change clothes."

One time in Rensselaer, Rick put bubble bath in the whirl-pool. Our trainer, Ed Rozy, went crazy. Until the day Ed died, he never knew Rick did it. He always suspected, but never knew. Rick would never tell him. The suds were coming out the door under the cracks into the gym. It was great.

We used to sneak out of camp once in a while. One time, Bo Farrington went out and came sneaking back in. He'd had a few. They locked the bottom door, so you had two options: you could climb up the side of the building to the second floor and try to get through a window up there or you could knock on a window downstairs. Bo chose downstairs and started knocking on a window. The guy that opened the window was George Allen. Bo just stepped right through the window and went through Allen's room. Of course, Allen told the Old Man.

When we were rookies, we went out and had a beer. When we sneaked back in, we ran into the guy we used to call "Silver Bullets," the guard they had. They would close the gates, but we got back in somehow and he turned a spotlight on us and was coming after us. We parked the car and jumped out and started running across the fields. They had fences, but all you could see were the poles. You couldn't see the piece of wire going from pole to pole. We were guessing when to jump. Mike Pyle hit the fence and had black and blue marks that were incredible. We sneaked into the cafeteria and somebody saw us. Of course, the only guy who got caught was Rick. He always got caught. Halas would say, "You have to name who was with you." Rick would never tell who was with him. Halas would say, "If you don't tell, you're going to get fined for everybody." So he would fine Rick $1,000 and we each had to pay him $250. Once I got fined $250 just for being out with Rick in Dallas. Halas said, "If you were out with Rick, you were up to no good."

The most fun anybody ever had was the weigh-in. They used to trick the scales. The Old Man would go crazy. One guy would get on the scale and another guy would put his finger under the cheek of his ass. Another guy would get on the scale with weights in his jock strap, so he would be heavier. It was a big Toledo scale and there was a way you could put a sponge under it that would cause you to be two or three pounds lighter. The Old Man would get down on his hands and knees and look underneath the scale. Or he would shake it. It was the funniest thing to watch. Halas supervised every weigh-in. Nobody weighed anybody in except him. He didn't trust anyone. We had to do it twice a week. It eventually got to the point that only certain guys had to weigh in. Poor Rick was one of them.

Rick was skinny at 230 and his weight was supposed to be 224 or 226. It was crazy. He couldn't get down. The fine was 25 bucks a pound. Know what it is today? Twenty-five bucks a pound. Does that make sense? The union restricts everything.

Halas used to have a players' committee to assess fines. Early in my career, I left my car in Rensselaer to go back to Chicago with someone else. Rick said, "Hey Mikey, Mikey baby, I'll take you back to camp."

I said, "O.K. Rick, where do I meet you?"

As soon as we met, I knew we weren't going back to camp. "Where are we going, Rick?"

"I got to make a stop in Gary, Indiana."

One thing led to another. We stopped. We missed the meal at camp. We stopped again and missed the meeting. We came roaring in there about 11 o'clock at night. The Old Man met us.

"You dirty bunch of so-and-so's," he said. Called us every name in the book. I was young, maybe my second year. He called me into his room and said, "What are you doing out whoring around?"

I said, "Coach, I had to ride back with Rick and we got detoured in Gary."

"You stupid S.O.B." he said.

At that time we had a players' committee made up of Bill George, Stan Jones, Fred Williams and a couple other guys. Larry Morris probably was there because he was sensible. Doug Atkins was there, too. I don't know how he got on the board, but he was on it. Rick's whole contention was the car broke down. Flat tire or something. So the Old Man said, "We'll go before the board." So we were pleading our case. The Old Man said, "I think they ought to be fined." Somebody on the board stood up and spoke for us. The Old Man said. "We'll put it to a vote." The board said, "Don't fine them. We think the car broke down."

Boy, did the Old Man get mad.

"O.K., that's the end of this board," he said. "You guys are disbanded."

He fined us anyway and that was the end of the board.

IX

Plays, Players, and "The Run"

You remember the people you were around and what you accomplished as a team longer than anything else. Some people remember me for the run I made in the game against Pittsburgh in 1963. Hell, that was the luckiest run in the world. It was a combination of me being tired, them being tireder, and poor tackling. It was terrible. I look at it and I'm amazed they think that was a good run. I made better runs than that. I made a run in Minnesota to get into the end zone after I got hit by a couple people. In Wrigley Field against the 49ers once I caught a pass over the middle and only went 20 or 25 yards, but I know I was hit by four or five guys and just kept bouncing off of them. It was not a run where I was going to go far, but I thought it displayed more running talent than the one in Pittsburgh. That was kind of a fluky thing, but everybody remembers it because it made the highlight films.

It was my first time back in Pittsburgh since college, so it was a big thing for my parents. But it was the same weekend after President John F. Kennedy was killed. It was a very disappointing time for our country and nobody wanted to play football. But once they said we had to play football, that was our job. It would have been double jeopardy to go out there and play a terrible football game.

It was really a good football game, a hard-played game. We were behind 17-14 and we were coming out of our own territory. Bill Wade was the quarterback and he threw a pass that a Pittsburgh linebacker named John Reger dropped for an interception that would have been a touchdown for them. We got somewhere out around the 20-yard line. I caught eight or nine passes that day and played the whole game, so I was tired. Bill wanted to call a deep route to me and I said, "Bill, I can't go deep. You throw me something short. I'll go down about 14 yards and hook. Then I'll try to run with it." I told him we didn't have to go all the way anyway. All he had to do was make a couple first downs and kick a field goal. So I caught the pass and the first guy who hit me was Clendon Thomas. He was the last guy who tackled me. In between, I don't know who hit me. I don't really remember very much about the run. I was tired. It went for 50 yards and we tied the game with a field goal 17-17.

Nobody remembers the greatest catch I ever made in football. You know why? It was the day Gale Sayers scored six touchdowns against the 49ers in Wrigley Field in 1965. I dove, hit the ball with one hand and brought it back and slid into the end zone for a touchdown. Rudy Bukich threw it and I told Rudy, "I'm making you look good, kid. Keep throwing to me." But Sayers went on his rampage and I never got a mention.

The only guy who got a mention was Jon Arnett, who scored another touchdown as Sayers' sub.

I really don't ever remember a best game I might have had. I probably remember some of the worst games. I scored four touchdowns against the Rams during that 1963 season, but the Rams were having trouble at that time and they weren't really a good team. There were some good catches, but somebody threw me the ball and somebody forgot to cover me and I was just running open. We won 52-14; it was a blowout. I made 13 catches against Washington in 1964 but we got beat. We threw the ball all day, but when you get beat, it doesn't mean anything.

One of the best games we had was in 1963 when we beat the Packers bad in Chicago. I don't know that I did anything in the game, but that was really a great feeling because that was really a team effort.

You remember the players more than the plays.

Sayers and Dick Butkus were both rookies in 1965. I remember when they came in, it wasn't all peaches and cream because you were ending an era when Butkus replaced Bill George. If you were in the George syndicate, you weren't a big Butkus fan. But whether you were a Butkus fan or not, when you watched him line up and play, then even Bill George was a Butkus fan. He was our kind of player. He was a Bear.

When Gale came in, he was sort of a bashful guy. So was Butkus. He wouldn't say two words. Gale was the same way and didn't really assert himself. Gale's first couple practices, I think he had a few nagging injuries, a hamstring or something. Everybody was watching Brian Piccolo, who was a free agent. Sayers and Butkus were the No. 1 draft choices and everybody couldn't believe how good Piccolo looked. I remember talking to Gale one day in Rensselaer. We walked from a practice field to the dining hall and I told him, "You're in the spotlight. A lot of people are going to judge you on what they see not only in games, but in practice." I told him, "These guys aren't any better than you. They can't even carry your jock. Just go out and do what you can do. Take your time to get well and you'll do fine."

Gale never really turned it on during the exhibition season. I think at first, a lot of guys wondered about his courage at times. But I don't think they wondered much after the season started. I think that's only natural. What happens sometimes when you come in as a first-round pick people wonder, "What right do you have to make that kind of money when I've played all these years?" Plus, they're going to take away one of your friend's jobs. So everybody sticks up for their friends. There were a lot who felt that way about me and then there were a lot who helped me. I think Bill George helped Butkus. I think once you saw these guys were super football players, you knew they would make us a much better football team.

Sayers showed flashes in the exhibition season, but he never showed what a complete player he was. He blocked. He was a hell of a receiver. He would have been a great outside receiver. He would have been like Charley Taylor with better moves than Charley, maybe not as strong as Charley. Sayers became a great receiver coming out of the backfield. He blocked well because we ran a lot of formations where he had to make a block for the fullback. There is no question when he accelerated through a hole, he was like he came out of a gun. And the thing that made him so amazing, even though he could accelerate, he could change direction. He had kind of an ability to hop and leap and he really was magic to watch run.

I remember one game, he made a move that was like one of those old Ozark Ike things you see in the comic strips. He was going down the sideline and there was a guy coming from behind, a guy coming from the front and a guy coming at him from the side. He planted and cut between two guys and it looked like all three of them hit together. It was the damndest thing I've ever seen. He went on for a touchdown. It was just incredible some of the runs he made.

The punt return against San Francisco in the mud on the day he scored six touchdowns was incredible. He was the only guy playing on a dry field that whole day because he had that flat-foot running ability. It looked like he was never on the side of his feet. He was always planting and squaring up. His center of balance was really good. I don't know if there will ever be a better one. I know there have been some great open field runners in the history of the game. Hugh McElhenny was great, but I don't think there was ever an open field runner like Sayers. I'm talking open field now. He was a great cutback runner and I don't ever remember him being caught.

I played against Butkus once as a Cowboy and once as an Eagle. I know for a fact he took it easy on me and I don't think he ever took it easy on anybody. He probably knew I was over the hill. He was the epitome of the middle linebacker. I'm not saying Dick was the greatest technically at what he did. To me, that has nothing to do with anything. If a guy is great technically, fine. You can learn to be good technically. But when you play the game the way he played it, you play to take no prisoners. He didn't give a shit who liked it or who didn't. He played the game from the tip of his head to the bottom of his soles. He just didn't care if you liked him or hated him. He would tell you right out of the box, "I'm going to get you. If I get a chance, I'm going to break your head." And that was it. Nitschke was about the same way. There was not much difference in those guys. Cut from the same mold.

Maybe if I would have been a defensive player, I would have played that way. Not on offense. On offense, you have to be intelligent. On defense, you just have to be brutal.

During the exhibition season in 1963, we played the Giants. We lost to them in 1962 and we played them the next year in the preseason. I don't care who they had playing. They were the Giants and they were good. We kicked their butts. I'll never forget. It was on a Saturday and that Sunday we were back in Rensselaer and Mr. Halas called me down to his room and said, "What do you think about this football team?" I said, "Coach, I think this team can win a championship." He said, "Why do you think that?" I said, "Well, I don't know how hard the Giants played, but I know we played very well. We have better personnel than the Giants have." He said, "You know, I think you're right. This could be a great year for the Bears." That's the truth. It was really one of the closest conversations we had about anything like that.

We had a good football team. Larry Morris, Rosey Taylor, Bennie McRae, Joe Fortunato. Joe was probably the most underrated guy. Ed O'Bradovich. If Ed hadn't been sick one year, he would have been an all-pro football player. Offensively, we kind of had a no-name team. Willie Galimore was a great running back. Casares and Joe Marconi were the fullbacks. Johnny Morris and Bo Farrington were the wide receivers. The line was Bob Wetoska, Herman Lee, Mike Pyle, Ted Karras, Mike Rabold and Jim Cadile. We were resourceful. We made a lot of first downs. Once we got to the 20s, we didn't get into the end zone too much. But we weren't a bad football team. I think the defense respected us and I know we respected the defense.

The one game I remember more than any was the Detroit game in 1963 that got us into the championship game. To me, that was better than the championship game because we were on the verge of getting beat. It was just a great feeling we had on the sideline, people rallying around each other. Detroit was a tough football team. They had us going pretty good that day and were starting to move the ball again and Davey Whitsell took a gutty chance and made an interception. He cut in front of Gail Cogdill on the sideline and went with it. If it's a sideline takeoff, the game's over, Detroit wins. But that's the way Dave played. He had to take risks because he didn't have all the speed in the world. That play was my biggest thrill in football and I wasn't even on the field. It excited me so much it was incredible. When I hear Jack Brickhouse's rendition, him and Kup on the radio, it's just amazing. It really was exciting. I don't think anything in the championship game when we beat the Giants 14-10 ever came near that much excitement. Not even O.B.'s great interception. Of course, O.B. thinks it did. I think what was exciting was Del Shofner not being able to catch the ball when he ran out of the sunlight into the shadow in the end zone. A sure touchdown and he was such a good receiver. That end of the field was frozen and I think he started slipping as he went into the end zone. I don't really remember the championship game nearly as well as I remember that Detroit game or some of the other games that year. Maybe I was a little too tense for the championship game.

I told our players in 1984 they had to make up their minds if the reward we're seeking is worth the price they were going to have to pay, because you have to pay a price. I just told them to make up their minds that the Super Bowl was worth it. It's hard to tell someone what the top of the mountain is like if they've never been on the mountain. I'd been on top twice and to the mountain a number of times. It's pretty good. All the bitching the Bears did in 1964 didn't matter. We still got that ring. We complained that Halas didn't reward us like the Packers got rewarded. We still got the recognition that we were the champions. Who was to know that it wasn't going to happen again for 22 years? That team will be remembered in this city longer than the Stanley Cup team, more than the last Cub team. An amazing thing. You hear people say, "I remember the '63 Bears." The reward will always be there.

In 1964, Willie Galimore and Bo Farrington were killed in a car accident in Rensselaer during training camp. The Olympics were on television that night and some of the guys had gone out to the Country Club to watch it. We were playing poker. Early in the morning, when I got up, I was in the bathroom. Joe Sullivan, the former St. Louis Cardinal general manager who worked with us then, was in the bathroom and he was crying. I said, "What's the matter?" He said, "Hasn't anybody told you? Bo and Willie were killed last night."

I said, "You're kidding. It can't be. I just left them." We had been out at the Country Club earlier messing around and we came back to play poker. There was a real funny road with a big S-curve in it coming back from the Country Club. They had mowed the grass that day and had taken down the warning sign. Evidently, they just went off the shoulder of the road. It was a high shoulder. They had a Volkswagen with a sun roof that was open. They must have swerved to get back on the road and the car flipped. The wheel broke completely off the car and flipped. Bo went out the roof. The car rolled over on Willie and broke his neck.

The shock was unbelievable. Rick, and Bill George and I went down to the morgue and saw them maybe 8 hours after it happened. I don't think the sadness ever left. I say sadness, but there was also disbelief that those two guys could be gone. They were always together, two of the most likeable guys you've ever seen. They were both great football players. In today's era, they would have been super. Galimore probably never got the credit he deserved, but I think if you compared him in speed with Sayers and Walter, there would be no comparison. Willie was faster. He could fly. He played after at least three knee surgeries. He could still cut and change directions incredibly well. It was amazing how good he was. In 1963, he had a great year and I think he was just coming back into his prime. Farrington was a 6-4, 212-pound receiver who could run. He was a long strider, a track guy, but he could still run and he had good hands.

I think that took a lot of wind out of our sails. We never really recovered from it.

X

Humility in Philadelphia

I dislocated my shoulder in 1964 and caught 75 passes that year wearing a harness. We were awful. All we could do was throw the ball. We were 5-9. In 1965, I hurt my foot. I played every game, but caught only 36 passes. We were 9-5 and should have won it all. The 1966 season was my last with the Bears. I caught only 32 passes and we had a record of 5-7-2.

I was traded to the Philadelphia Eagles in 1967. I'm sure if there is such a thing as purgatory on earth, I was in it there. Not that they served it on me; I served it on myself. I just spent it in Philadelphia. It was the low point of my life. I really drank a lot. Almost killed myself drinking.

Nobody would ever say I am a Philadelphia Eagle or a

Dallas Cowboy. That's a fact of life. I was always a Bear.
That's how people perceive me. Just like Butkus could never
have been a San Diego Charger. He was a Chicago Bear. That's
it. I say the same thing about Doug Atkins. He wasn't a Cleveland Brown or a New Orleans Saint. He was a Chicago Bear.
Bill George was never an L.A. Ram. He was a Chicago Bear.
There were certain people who were Chicago Bears, period.
Halas looked for those kind of people. Maybe he didn't always
find them, but then if he couldn't find them, he'd change
them. That's why I was a Bear and when I left I was still a
Bear. And it hurt. I caused it all. I could have stopped it.

After the 1965 season, the American Football League
called me. Don Klosterman of the Oilers offered me $300,000
for three years, including a $50,000 signing bonus and a lot on
a golf course in Houston. This was all for the 1967 season. I
was going into my option year with the Bears in 1966.

Klosterman said he would meet me in Chicago. I called a
lawyer friend of mine, Lester Marshall, and we agreed to
terms. They got me on the phone with Al Davis, who was commissioner of the AFL. He said, "You want to do what you're
doing?" I said, "Yep." I signed and Klosterman gave me a
check for $50,000 right on the spot. I denied later that I had
signed, but I lied. It was the height of the war between the
NFL and AFL.

I had been negotiating with Mugs Halas because the Old
Man wouldn't even talk about it. It came down to where the
contract offers were pretty close. Instead of $250,000, the
Bears would have paid me maybe $200,000 over three years.
But I didn't sign. I decided to play out my option with the
Bears for the 1966 season.

The money wasn't really that big a deal. They knew I was
talking to the AFL. The one thing I told Mr. Halas was, "I
played all these years for you and I played hard. I've not always
been everything you wanted, but I played hard. Here's the

Houston Oilers, people I've never played one down for, and they want to pay me this kind of money. They put a value on me of this much, and you don't put the same value on me." That's the only thing I never could understand. It bothered me.

I understand a lot of the players' positions today because some salaries are so goofy it throws everything out of whack. When I was out breaking my ass making $12,000 and we had a second or third-string quarterback making $25,000, you tend to think, "What the hell's going on? This doesn't make sense." I probably asked Mr. Halas about it and he probably gave me a great explanation, which appeased me and I walked away and said, "uh-uh, he must be right," and scratched my head. But I never understood it.

When Butkus and Sayers came in 1965, their contracts didn't bother me at all. I don't think I knew what they were. But after that season, when that offer came from Houston, I thought, "Gees, these people get this kind of money playing football?" That was pretty hard to believe. A $250,000 contract for three years plus a $50,000 signing bonus got your attention if you were making $25,000. After playing five years in Chicago, they thought I was worth $25,000 and somebody else thought I was worth $100,000. I started thinking something was out of whack.

In retrospect, I understand it better now because I think it was a matter of Mr. Halas never going to get caught in a position of saying, "Hey, I really need you." He wouldn't get caught in that position with Bill George or Doug Atkins or myself or anybody else. That's just the way it was. He probably never would have got totally caught in that position even with Butkus. He had seen too many players come and go. He had seen the greatest. The Osmanskis, the Kavanaughs, Beattie Feathers.

Shortly after I signed with the AFL, the leagues merged. John Brodie, Roman Gabriel, Jim Taylor and some other guys had talked to the AFL like me. The league picked up the contracts, so Halas knew I had signed.

When I played out my option then in 1966, the Bears cut my salary 10 percent. Those were the rules then when you played out your option. They never really cut anybody the 10 percent, but they cut me the 10 percent.

It was before 1966 that I made the remark about Halas throwing around nickels like they were manhole covers. I can't even remember the details. I think it was at a banquet. I do know I didn't originate it. I probably heard it from Bill George or Fred Williams. I'll tell you one thing: you couldn't say much in Chicago that Mr. Halas didn't know about. It would come back to him from somewhere. He had a really powerful network of people that had great respect for him. I don't think anybody would come back and tell him something just to try to get me in trouble. They just wanted him to know exactly what was going on with everybody. I get the same thing from people now myself, but what the players say today is their business. Sometimes it upsets me inside, but it wouldn't bother me outside anymore.

I played all those years and that's what they remember me for—one statement that the old man tossed around nickels like they were manhole covers. It made Halas furious when he found out about it. I said, "You know better than that. I was just kidding when I said it." He said, "Well, you know that's true anyway."

The thing that really made him mad was once I called him a cheap Bohemian. He came right to me. I was getting dressed and he called me in and asked me about it, but I said I just said it in jest. I told him I could have called him a cheap S.O.B. but the Bohemian thing was something I was just being cute with.

He said, "Don't be cute with my nationality."

I said, "It's like you saying that I'm a dumb Polack or something. Why would that bother me?" He was right, though. It was a stupid thing to say. Those are things you do when you're young and trying to be cute.

One time, Johnny Morris and I went to a banquet for Allied Chemical. It was a luncheon on an off day in 1965 and someone from the audience asked who the quarterback should be. Johnny said Rudy Bukich and I said Rudy. Bill Wade was still the quarterback. We went into elaborations of strengths and weaknesses between Rudy and Bill. Ray Sons was in the audience and he wrote the article for the Daily News. At about 1 o'clock in the morning, I was home in bed and I got a phone call. It's Halas and he's just reaming me out, just killing me. "You get down here and see me."

I said, "It's late, I didn't do anything. I'll come down and see you first thing in the morning. I'll come in before practice. I'll come by the office." He was calling me every name in the book. Did the same thing with Johnny. He made us get up and apologize to the whole team.

I said, "Coach, I didn't do anything wrong." John got up and apologized. He said if he did any harm, he was sorry because the team was important. I stood up and said, "I can't apologize because I didn't do anything wrong." I said, "Nothing means more to me than football or this team, so I don't think I've done anything wrong regardless of what Mr. Halas says."

I just said it was against my nature to apologize for something I didn't do. The story was really nothing; it was just the way it hit Mr. Halas. He didn't say very much, probably called me an S.O.B. I don't think he was very happy. But I think it would have been the same thing he would have done.

I say it doesn't bother me what players say. Some of it bothers me. What they say about me personally doesn't bother me, but any time they detract from the team or the organization, it does bother me a little bit. The Bears are not a cheap organization. I think they're trying to be a smart organization in the way they handle business. I don't know if that's always right or wrong. I know somewhere sanity has to prevail in sports and I think we're trying to be sane about what we're doing, period. That bothers me when they say the Bears are cheap. They're not. We do things first class and we always have. It was the same when I played. We stayed at the best places. We stayed in the Palace in San Francisco, and all the best places, because I think Mr. Halas enjoyed that.

My attitude never changed my last year playing with the Bears. Nobody could ever say I didn't play as hard or I didn't practice as hard. That would be a lie. I played every game like it was my last game. I got a little disgruntled when I couldn't get the ball thrown to me. I gained some weight because I was blocking more. But I never changed. I really felt the quarterbacks were told not to throw me the ball, because I was open a lot that last year and caught only 32 passes and only two touchdowns. The films show that I was open. I guess I kind of started to feel sorry for myself. I had caught a lot of passes before and I just felt that my talent wasn't being utilized the way it had been.

I said we won in spite of management and the coaches. I didn't really mean it about the coaches. I got a lot out of guys like Luke Johnsos and Phil Handler and Chuck Mather. My mouth was operating before my brain got in gear. I do think the Bears went through some goofy times for no reason. There were some pretty good football players around who weren't happy and weren't working enthusiastically within the system. Our overall attitude back then was not good.

Halas and I argued on the field some. I remember an Armed Forces exhibition game against the Cardinals when they beat the hell out of us. I don't know if I had a great game or a bad game, but after they dissected the film, they noticed I wasn't running the routes the way they wanted them run. The next day on the field, Halas made an example out of me. I got in a little argument. I said, "You have to make the adjustment off the man. You can't always run the exact depth you guys have drawn up. You can't put chalk marks out there and run routes that way all the time during a game." He really got mad about that. He said, "You run them this depth."

Before my next-to-last game with the Bears, we went to San Francisco and Halas timed a meeting at 8 o'clock, which the coach is going to do if he's smart. If someone was going to go out and start doing something, he was going to be at the meeting at 8 o'clock and have no time to do anything afterwards. A lot of guys were griping and they came to me. I asked Halas why we didn't have the meeting as soon as we got there so the players could go eat and then get checked at curfew. But he knew exactly what he was doing. I was quoted as saying I had a "personality conflict" with Halas. I was just talking with the mentality of a 27-year-old player. Just rhetoric. Words. Just making an out for myself. "Personality conflict."

I think up until the last second, I could have stopped the trade. It would have been different if I had been a guy who always bitched and never played. I did bitch, but I liked to practice and I played hard. I can't apologize for that to anybody and Halas knew that. That's why I'm here today. He knew there were some things that happened, but he knew my attitude toward football was always good. Always good, whether I came in with a hangover or not. I had more fun on the field than most of these guys.

I'm sure something could have been worked out for me to stay in Chicago. But a trade became very appealing to the Bears once they found out they could get Jack Concannon. They were looking for a little more stability at quarterback. They knew I had gone through a bad foot injury and my speed had dropped off a little bit. They didn't know how much production they were going to get out of me. I was in the hospital to have more work done on my foot when Mugs came to see me. He said, "What do you think?" I said, "I think it's up to you. If you want to make a trade, do it."

I cried like hell when I left even though I created the leaving. I was leaving friends, going to another city. Life wasn't any fun for me. But it was important that it happened. I really believe there is a plan for everybody's life. I'm not saying it's predestination. I just say you are put in certain places for certain reasons. Life teaches lessons. I think I was put in Philadelphia for a reason. That reason was to learn a little humility in life. It was a drop. It was like going from the penthouse to the outhouse. It was not that I didn't enjoy playing in Philadelphia; it was just a big setback for me.

The league paid the contract I had signed with the Oilers. I never got that kind of money anyway. All I did was defer the money until I retired and took it over a period of 10 years. I never got a big salary. The highest salary I ever played for in pro football was $44,000 in Dallas my last year.

The first year in Philadelphia wasn't bad. I looked at it as a new opportunity. I was starting anew and I really looked forward to the challenge.

I got involved in a hurry. We played the New York Jets in Cincinnati in the third preseason game in 1967 and Johnny Sample hit Timmy Brown out of bounds, which was where Sample usually hit people. So I ran over and got into a little tussle with him and they threw both of us out of the game. A guy asked me afterwards what I thought and I said, "I just think he's a garbage can." That's all I said. I didn't retract it then and I don't retract it now. I don't care what he thinks of me or I think of him. I just know he played the game outside the rules, period. He wasn't tough enough to do that. There were guys who could play outside the rules and were tough enough to back it up, but he wasn't. He wouldn't do anything to your face. He would do it when you weren't looking. That I didn't like.

We ended up 6-7-1 that first year, 1967, and beat the Cowboys. We weren't that bad a football team. But the next year, we came back and it was like all hell broke loose.

We were supposed to play our first exhibition game in Mexico City against Detroit and they had a revolution down there and cancelled it. So we played the game in Franklin Field in Philadelphia. The field had not had any water on it for three months. It was like playing on the sidewalk. I tore a ligament or tendon completely off my heel. Really painful. Our quarterback, Norm Snead, broke his ankle. After the game, Frank Gifford was interviewing me. He asked what I thought. The only thing I said was: "Before you can win, there has to be a winning attitude that permeates from top to bottom." I said everybody had to be infected with the idea of winning. You can't just say the players have to be infected. Everybody does. The Eagles took it kind of wrong and they really got on me about it. I never really played a whole lot more after that. They even waived me, but too many teams claimed me and they took me off the waiver list.

We finished 2-12 after starting out 0-11. Other guys got hurt. There was a lot of turmoil. The club was in disarray. The owner, Jerry Wolman, had financial problems. I really had a hard time dealing with anything. The coach was Joe Kuharich and I don't think there was anything wrong with him or the coaching staff. I just think we got into a situation where we were expected to win and didn't. I saw a whole different way a club was run. I saw guys who were catered to because they were prima donnas. I saw others who played hard but weren't catered to. I saw people with thin skin when you were trying to say something to improve the ball club.

The whole year was a real low point for me. I was by myself. I had an apartment in downtown Philadelphia. My family was still in Chicago. Basically, every night I would go out. I really drank a lot. I wasn't playing and it was just ridiculous. I was about trying to kill myself with the drinking. I was in bad shape. Nothing else to do. I was a mess. I never felt good the whole year. You wonder why you pull muscles. My God, you pull muscles if you're full of alcohol. You pull muscles because it dehydrates you.

Even though I would have good intentions of going out and having dinner, I would start drinking. I would always say I was going out to eat and would be back in the apartment at 8 o'clock at night. But I know I woke up in some strange places, not knowing how I got there or why I was there or who I was with or anything like that. I could have been in Alabama as well as Philadelphia. I would go through the day after like I was in a fog, not being able to distinguish between what was real and what wasn't real. I just know things weren't going good and I wasn't playing much and I was in the doghouse. So I just went through the motions. I always did try to practice hard. That's one thing I didn't shortchange them on. But I wanted to escape from it and the escape was to go back to a restaurant or a bar and that was it.

I couldn't afford champagne at that time. I think I was doing some pretty good whiskey. I don't remember. Whiskey, beer, wine, whatever was available. I can remember my skin, my complexion, everything changed. I got goofy. I really did for a long time. It was just a very unusual thing. It wasn't that I woke up and looked forward to doing it. It could have become addictive, but it didn't. It really hurt me physically and mentally. When you get into that situation, you lose confidence and I think it's partly because you lose self-respect. That's basically what happened. There was a lot of self-pity involved.

Late in the season, we went to New York to play the Giants. We lost 7-6 and were 0-10. Gary Ballman and I were asked to stay over and speak at a function. There were some questions asked. It was no secret we weren't a very good football team if we were 0-10. We told the usual banquet jokes. We used to say when the coach was penalized 15 yards for yelling from the sidelines it was unnecessary. Five yards was plenty for the way he was coaching. Ballman said he was going to have some cufflinks made up with an Eagle on them and have our record engraved underneath. That really made Kuharich mad and he suspended both of us. I said, "O.K." And I took it for a day. Then I went in and talked to him and I was reinstated.

He said we'd bury the hatchet and let bygones be bygones. We went to Cleveland to play and he said I would play a lot in the game. He played me as a token. I didn't play much at all. It was really embarrassing. My parents had come up. I told them not to. I was sitting on the bench and I just started thinking about it, saying what a mess I created. What a bullshit mess. And I cried. It just brought me to tears. I really didn't blame Joe or anybody else, because I don't think anybody got me in my predicament except me. I don't say that anybody else was wrong. But when you're young, the one thing you don't do is ever blame yourself. It's too hard to do. You're looking for people to blame. "God damn, it would have been a lot better if this guy wouldn't have done this or coach wouldn't have done that." Sure, it would have been better. But what if you hadn't put yourself in that predicament? What if you hadn't done what you'd done? Looking back, I don't blame anybody. At that time, I'm sure I blamed everybody.

The thing I learned is you better understand that you're only passing through this life. You've only got a lease on it. You don't own it. If you put too much self-importance in your value and who you are and how important you are, you're going to find out that there's going to be somebody else who's going to come along who's a little more important who is going to do the job a little better. I learned that they wouldn't have done any better or any worse whether I was on the field or not.

I learned humility. I dug a pretty deep hole and I was in the son of a gun and I wasn't figuring out how to get the hell out of it very well. My car was packed when we played the Vikings in the last game. There was snow up to your ass. When the game was over, I must have worn my clothes underneath my uniform because I was undressed and down the stairs. I didn't say goodby, hello, or anything. I was in my car and I drove nonstop except for gas through a blizzard across Pennsylvania and through Ohio, Indiana, and into Chicago. I knew I wasn't going back to Philadelphia. I had pretty much made up my mind I wasn't going to play any more. I had another year on my contract, but it wasn't worth it.

XI

We Hated the Cowboys

Three or four days after I got home from Philadelphia, I got a phone call from Tom Landry. Out of the blue. He said, "We don't even know if you can play anymore, but we're going to bring you down and take a look at you and see if you can play a few years." He said they already had a tight end, Pettis Norman, and they were really happy with him. "We think you can complement him," he said.

I had been dead serious about retiring. I couldn't play a lick. But the Cowboys traded for me anyway. Sent Dave Mc-Daniel, the burner, to the Eagles. He was the receiver who had such a fast time in the 40-yard dash until they found out the field was short. Anyway, I couldn't understand why they traded for me. Looking back, I was traded for a reason. The

Good Lord put me there. At that time, I couldn't really understand why it was the Cowboys or why it was Landry. But life is cycles and that was the start of a new cycle and it turned out to be an upbeat cycle.

It wasn't all roses in the beginning there, either. I really wasn't crazy about going there until I got there. I had never liked the Cowboys. When I played, if you played for the Bears or the Eagles, you didn't like the Cowboys, that's for sure. They were the good guys. They were the guys in white hats. They had the stars. They were good. When I was with the Eagles, I remember our running back, Timmy Brown, came across the middle and the Cowboys' middle linebacker, Lee Roy Jordan, gave him a shot and knocked out his uppers, lowers, everything. Timmy had about $2,500 worth of teeth in his mouth. When we had a beer after the game, he was drinking through cotton. He had to go right to the orthodontist. He was a mess. Lee Roy had hit him right across the chops with a good forearm. So I was trying to go after Lee Roy the rest of the game. I don't know that I ever got there, but I tried. Lee Roy became a good friend and I could understand why Lee Roy played the way he played. He played the way I played. He played tough and aggressive and went after people. That was O.K. with me, but when you were on the other side of the ball, then you had to go after that guy.

There was always bad blood between the Eagles and the Cowboys. We hated them and they hated us worse than anybody. Well, you don't hate anybody worse than the Redskins. There were some great rivalries in that division. Dallas and Washington. Dallas and St. Louis. Dallas and New York. It's a tough division for rivalries. Everybody enjoyed playing Dallas. They enjoyed playing against Dallas more than they enjoyed playing against Pittsburgh when the Steelers were winning. When people played Pittsburgh, they didn't know what they were getting into. But they always could understand a little about what they were getting into when they played Dallas. They always had the idea that beating Dallas would make them a star on America's flag or something.

But when I got to the Cowboys and met them and saw them, I realized they were just like anybody else. A great bunch of guys. That's a lot of the reason they were a good football team. They were good players on the field and good guys off the field. You could go out and have a beer with them and they had fun. I thought that was a lot of the reason they won. It wasn't that much different. They bitched about Tom just like the Packers bitched about Lombardi and the Bears bitched about Halas and the Browns bitched about Brown. It's never different. If they don't bitch about the coach, I guess something's got to be goofy.

My first season there, 1969, was kind of a funny year. Not much happened. I got in some fights when we scrimmaged the Rams and the Chargers. I didn't play much that first year except in short yardage and goal line. I couldn't ever understand that. In our sixth game that year, we were beating the hell out of the Giants and I wasn't playing very much. In the fourth quarter, Tom called me to go in and I just said, "No point in me going in now." And I wouldn't go in. Next day, he called me into the office and said, "If that ever happens again, just take off the uniform and go."

I said, "O.K." That's really the way I felt, because it didn't really matter to me the first year whether I stayed or left anyway. I wasn't that worried about it. Didn't bother me at all. But it never happened again. I started playing more. The other guy, Norman, was a good blocker, but I was a good blocker, too. I wasn't in good shape my first year, so I wasn't going to beat him out the first year. But it didn't bother me because I really didn't give a damn.

After we got beat by Cleveland in the playoffs, I said to myself, "Hey, this is a good football team, as good as anybody." I made up my mind I was going to get in the best shape of my life or kill myself trying. And I did. I moved down there and lived down there and I worked out every day. I got into their offseason training program. Because of my bad foot, I started running barefoot. I'd run in the grass.

Alvin Roy, who was their strength coach, had a system. You lifted, then you ran a hundred down the field and a hundred back. Then you lifted another set and ran again. You could hardly move your legs. But this was how the Cowboys tested the players coming into camp. I think that year only Roger Staubach and Calvin Hill had better times than I did. I was in pretty good shape for a guy my age. That was in 1970, when I turned 31. I was in the best shape I ever got in my whole life regardless of the foot injury. Both 1970 and 1971 were Super Bowl years. The 1971 season was the best year I ever played.

That conditioning program enabled me to do it and I always thought the big edge the Cowboys had was so many guys lived in Dallas. Guys in Chicago and Philadelphia always had their cars packed and they were leaving. In Dallas, very few left. The climate was conducive for staying and the opportunities in the town were phenomenal. I think Landry's conditioning system was patterned after Lombardi's. He could tell the people who would pay the price during the offseason—Dan Reeves, Walt Garrison, that kind of player. Rayfield Wright was as good a tackle as I've seen. Dave Edwards. Whoever heard of Dave Edwards except the guys who played against him? A heck of a football player. Cornell Green switched from corner to safety and became the best safety in the league. He always had people like that. Those guys always paid the price. Any player today who doesn't understand the benefits of the offseason conditioning program is foolish. I had never really lifted weights before. There's a lot of ways to get in shape and as you get stronger physically, you get stronger mentally.

I thought Landry was going to be kind of a sterile guy. I had a preconceived idea he was going to be a very sterile person. Maybe that's not the right word. I just thought he would be a plain guy with a lot of authority and not much emotion. I was completely wrong. I think Tom has as much emotion and compassion as anybody. I saw it in meetings we had, but I saw it more when I became a coach. You really saw what made him work and what made him tick. You saw how bad he felt when he cut people.

People say he's cold. He's the furthest thing from cold. But what is he going to do? Sidle up to everybody buddy-buddy and go out and have a beer with them? You can't do that. The "plastic" image was something that came out to the public, but it certainly wasn't the truth. That bothered him. In staff meetings, we saw the personality, the friendship, the jokes and laughter. We played golf with him. Other people don't see that part of him. They just see the guy on the sideline calling the plays, wearing the hat, the guy who doesn't smile a lot.

We laughed at the way he murdered names. Pete Retzlaff was Rexlaff, Joe Scarpati was Scarpeter. He didn't call his own quarterback Gary Hogeboom. It came out Hogenboomer or Haagen-Dazs or whatever he happened to say. He does not do it on purpose. The Cowboys used to bring in over 100 rookies. Tom would call out the names and they'd have to stand up. Every once in a while, there would be a Wisniewski or a Kurzawski and it was just a holy terror to hear him say it. And he would say, "Correct me if I'm saying it wrong." The guy would say it right and Tom would say it again wrong. The guy would say it again right and Tom would say it again wrong. That was no reflection on how he felt about his players, though. You think coaches just cut people, that they enter into their lives and walk out of their lives. Coaches feel as bad as players in most cases.

We used to have to grade and evaluate our players every

day. That way, we had a record so when it came time to cut, there was no question. The bottom guy had to go. It substantiated that you were cutting for no reason but lack of talent. And he tried to draw everything he could out of players. One time we cut a kid, Kenny Hutcherson, who was really a hitter, an inside linebacker who reminds me of Mike Singletary. He had been with us for one year and we had to cut him. It really shook Tom up. He broke down and he told the team, "I don't like this. But I have to do it because I think it's best for the team. That means I'll do it to anybody if I think they're a detriment to the team."

I knew when I saw that, boy, it had to be tough. Then when you go through it yourself, you know it's tough. People say after a couple of years it gets easy. I don't know what gets easy about it. I dread cutdown dates. Most kids know and accept it all right. Some don't accept it. I just try to tell them it's the decision of a lot of people. It's always a numbers game.

The four years I played in Dallas were difficult years for pro football. Think about what was coming out of college in 1969 and 1970. Think about what was going on then on college campuses. Everything was radical. Nobody wanted the Vietnam thing. Everybody had their own philosophies. Everybody was against the government. It was a different breed of person coming out. I had been playing pro ball for a while and seeing all kinds of guys come in. Then all of a sudden we got that smell around the locker room. We would say, "What the hell's that smell?" Then we got to understand more about it. I never knew what marijuana was. I never heard of it. I don't know what it was called when I grew up. I guess it was called hemp or rope. I never knew what it was. But I knew what it was in 1970. I smelled it everywhere.

Duane Thomas was the Cowboys' first-round draft choice in 1970. We knew he had some problems, but we thought the problems could be worked out because we thought he was a catalyst and he could get us to the Super Bowl. I don't think people realized what the problems were. They just thought he was unusual. They didn't know drugs might be involved. Nobody wanted to talk about drugs back then. They understood there was marijuana around, but nobody really talked about it.

Duane Thomas was a mixed-up kid, but he was an intelligent mixed-up kid. He was no dummy. He perceived anybody who wasn't a flower child as being part of the establishment and the establishment was wrong. It was a different group coming up. Duane, Steve Kiner, Tody Smith, Billy Parks, guys with talent, but they were fighting the cause of who knows what they were fighting. They were arguing every day about Vietnam and this and that. Sure, it's fine to have an opinion, but they used to drive poor Roger Staubach nuts. He'd just spent four years in the Navy.

When they were told something, it was always, "Why? Show me this is the best way." They questioned everything. They even questioned what Tom told them. It became a very, very tough situation.

The worst anguish Tom ever went through was with Duane Thomas. I've never seen a man suffer in trying to do what he thought was best for a football team, for the individual, and for everybody concerned. It was very agonizing and tough for Tom, but he did it. We won a Super Bowl, but it was pure hell in dealing with the way Thomas treated everybody. He treated his teammates no differently than he treated the press or he treated Tom or he treated everybody. He was just a real insensitive person, but he was very mixed up at that time. When you're dealing with what he was dealing with, you've got problems. Duane is basically a good guy.

Landry never really bent the rules for Thomas, but I think he bent himself a little bit. He tried to keep the rules standard for everybody. Duane was on time for meetings, but he never talked. He never had conversations with anybody. I don't even know that he ever talked to the coaches, really. He never answered roll call. He would be in the room, but he never said, "Here." Things like that. I think Tom made some concessions in that area. He did it because he thought it was best for the football team. After he did it, I'm not sure he believed he could ever make those concessions again with anybody.

Duane Thomas was a big factor in us winning. He was a good football player. He was a good all-around receiver, runner, blocker. He was a fluid runner who never took a real hard hit. He was like Jim Brown. He knew how to give and go, slip and slide, and all that stuff. He was an excellent blocker, which people didn't know about. Dan Reeves worked with him and said, "That guy is really smart." He knew the fullback and the halfback spots. He had to know both because Walt Garrison got hurt and Duane had to go up to fullback with Calvin Hill at halfback. But it was just uncomfortable to be around him, no fun.

Once we were playing the Giants in Yankee Stadium. I always made a habit of going up and wishing everybody good luck before a game. I went up to him and just patted him on the back and said, "Good luck." He didn't acknowledge it. I went on my way. We played the game. The following Tuesday, I was sitting beside my locker reading the paper in Dallas before practice and he came up to me and said, "Hey man, don't ever hit me on the back before a game. It breaks my concentration."

I said, "Hey Duane. Go fuck yourself."

That was our conversation.

Thomas only played for two years with the Cowboys. Then he was traded to New England and they gave him back. Then he was traded to San Diego and Washington and ended up in the World Football League. It was a shame because he could have been a real excellent football player for a long time, because he had the body for it and he had the temperament for it. But he blew himself out.

You've got to keep everything in society in perspective, though. When I played, amphetamines were accepted because they were given out by the team doctor. Now, amphetamines are barred and I agree they should be barred. I agree that steroids should be barred, but people have used steroids for years not really knowing what the consequences are, just like people have used cortisone for years. What are the consequences of cortisone? Does anybody really know? Is that the reason I have an artificial hip now? Might be. From all the cortisone injections I've taken, it might be. You don't know, but it was injected into me with the idea of improving the healing process. Doctors told me that.

I disagree with all drugs and any form of them, although it amazes me that alcohol is legal and acceptable but drugs aren't. I took amphetamines when I played with the Bears. They were handed to me. I didn't know what the hell they were. They said they'd make you play better or run faster or jump higher. I'd take them and I never saw any difference. Well, a couple of times I did. The first thing I noticed was warming up I would get extremely tired. I would feel like I was drained. Then I would get my energy back. Then at the end of the game, you'd have two beers and you were up on top of the roof. I did it a couple of times and that was it. I quit doing it. I became exposed to marijuana in Dallas, but I'm not a smoker, I can't inhale. I smoke cigars, but I can't inhale. I could have more fun drinking a couple beers than anything else.

I came to Dallas just as Pete Gent was leaving. I played with the same guys he wrote about in *North Dallas Forty* and I never saw the things he described. Maybe I wasn't at the same parties. I had as much fun there as I've had anywhere. I thought Dallas was going to be completely different from what

I pictured. I figured they would be a bunch of goody-goody guys, but they were super people, good football players who enjoyed themselves. They knew when to play, when to practice, and when to have fun. Gent wrote that a lot of football players in general don't particularly like each other. I find that hard to believe. To be a good team, the players have to like each other. They have to respect each other. They don't have to go out together and eat and drink together. Their wives don't have to socialize, but there has to be something there.

I didn't quite make the level of hell-raiser, but I was probably in tune with the guys who were. We didn't condone everything that was done, but we never said anything against it. We kind of went along with things. I think that's probably worse than being the guy who says, "Let's go do this." We'd say, "It doesn't make much sense to do it, but let's go ahead and do it anyway." So someone would say, "We're going to sit down and drink a shot of Wild Turkey for every year Walt Garrison had a birthday." And we'd start doing it. Garrison used to have a birthday party at training camp in Thousand Oaks every year. Used to get after that Wild Turkey. We would have a few shots and then start dancing. Dan Reeves had a staple in his knee. He started dancing and that staple came loose and we thought somebody shot him in the leg. We had to take him to the hospital. We had injuries dancing.

The first year I came to the Cowboys we were playing gin one night. Dan likes to tell this story on me. He said after I lost a few hands, I took a chair and threw it and it stuck in the wall. All four legs stuck in the wall. All Dan said was, "God, this guy must hate to lose." I'm not sure it happened exactly that way, but I'm not sure it didn't.

It was in Dallas where I got most of my nicknames. In college, they called me "Hammer" from my basketball days. I did bang people. In Dallas, Walt Garrison started calling me

Tie helps. *Ditka on sidelines during the 1985 season, game plans in hand. The tie helps rein in the temper.*
(Photo by Jonathan Daniel)

(Opposite page, top) *Just asking.* Ditka strikes
a rhetorical pose during dispute with officials
as Bears play New Orleans Saints in 1983.

(Opposite page, bottom) *New phase.* Ditka the actor
in a television commercial for American Express.

Wrong end. Head Coach Ditka warms up
during Bear practice. Showing players
is better than telling them.
(Photo by Jonathan Daniel)

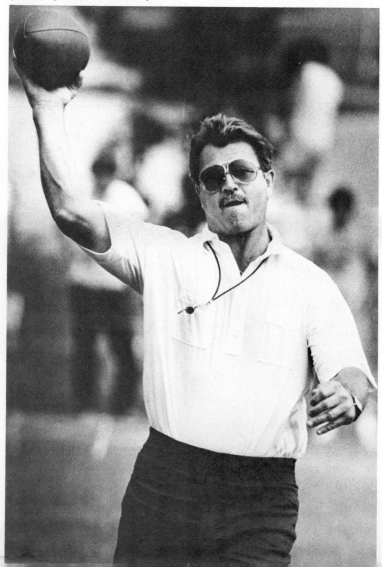

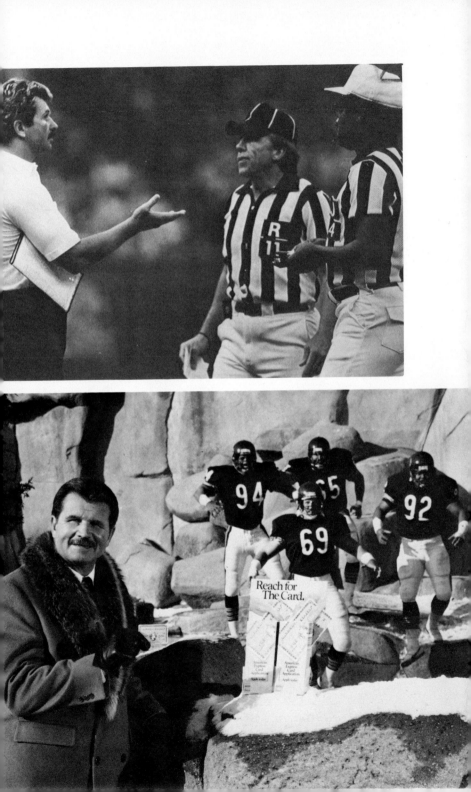

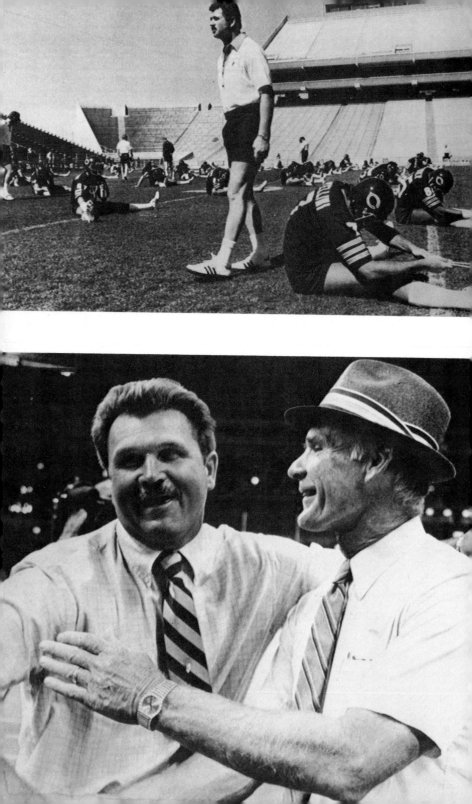

(Opposite page, top) *You play as you practice.*
Ditka supervises stretching exercises
during warmup drills in 1982.

(Opposite page, bottom) *Congrats. Ditka and Dallas*
Coach Tom Landry enjoy a brief post-game
reunion after the Cowboys beat the Bears 15-13
in a Monday night preseason
game at Irving, Texas, August 27, 1985.

(Below) *Not now. Everybody's not a nice guy on Sunday*
around 5 o'clock when things aren't going good.
(Photo by Jonathan Daniel)

Smooth swing. "Golf is a humbling game."

"I was always a Bear."

New coach. *The game plan is complete, said a triumphant George Halas, as he introduced new head coach Mike Ditka at a press conference on January 21, 1982.*

Brothers and sister. *Ashton,* (left) *and Michael stand behind Mary Ann and David in Aliquippa, PA.*

(Below) *Michael and Mom. Together nineteen years later in 1959.*

The Aliquippa smile. *Mike Ditka at 10 months and 10 days—August 28, 1940.*

High school. *A standout at Aliquippa High in football* (above) *(no. 80) and in basketball* (below) *(no. 6, front row center).*

*Priceless moment. At 20, Mike shares
his All America awards with his mother.*

(Opposite page)
The hammer. Cartoon summarizes some of the "Pitt" college achievements of punter-blocker-tackler-receiver-captain Ditka.

Round ball. With the Dallas Cowboys' basketball team in the early 1970s.

Brothers. Mike, 20, and Ashton, 19, admire Mike's college lineman of the year award.

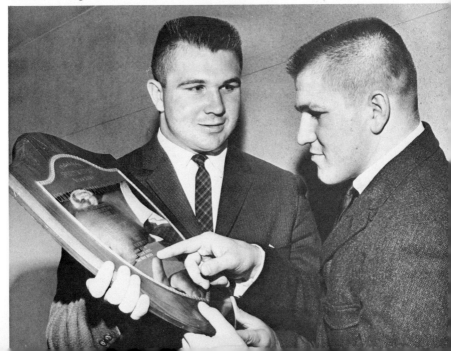

No. 89. Ready to go for the University of Pittsburgh in 1960.

Glint. The Ditka intensity
comes through the face mask
as a Dallas Cowboy on the
sidelines alone and
with Head Coach Tom Landry.
(Courtesy Dallas Cowboys)

Receiver corps. *Ditka* (left) *with Dallas wide receiver Bob Hayes* (center) *and flanker Lance Alworth, a few days before the Super Bowl meeting with the Miami Dolphins.*

Tough customer. *Ditka picks up steam after catching a pass against the Dolphins in Super Bowl VI.*
(Courtesy Dallas Cowboys)

Assistant Coach. *A slimmed down Ditka makes a point with all-pro Randy White during a Dallas Cowboy game in 1977.* (Courtesy Dallas Cowboys)

Kids. (from left) *Mike, Mark, Megan and Matt with their father during the Dallas days.*

At home. Mike and his wife, Diana, in their back yard.

All together. (Back row from left) *sons Mark, Matt, and Mike;* (front from left) *Debbie Jo (son Mike's wife), daughter Megan, Diana, and Charlotte Ditka (Mike's mom).*

"Monk" and "Chip" because I had chubby cheeks like a chip-monk.

Playing on the Cowboys' first two Super Bowl teams in 1970 and 1971 and scoring a touchdown in their first Super Bowl victory were highlights. I scored the final touchdown of our 24-3 win over Miami. Roger threw another touchdown pass to Duane Thomas, but I was wide open. I always told Roger if he had thrown the ball to me the first time, I would have won the car. When they honored all the MVP's at Super Bowl XX, I was going to tell him if he had thrown the ball to me, I would have been walking out there. I really should have scored three touchdowns. I ran a reverse and I really thought I had scored. I ran into my own lineman and misjudged the goal line.

You think it's going to last forever. You just figure the Good Lord gave you this body and it's going to keep working that way and it's not going to get hurt. You're going to wake up every day with enough enthusiasm to say, "Yeah, I'm going to play the game." All of a sudden, after you've been doing it for eight or nine years, even if you are healthy, then the mind starts playing tricks on you. It makes it tough. You start saying, "I don't know if I'm going to catch that one coming inside. I got hurt last time." You start to think, "If I can get through this year, maybe I can get through another year." It's the security you get in football. You get used to the good life, get used to the adulation, where people put you on a pedestal. The thing that's important is to be realistic about your talents. It's easy to say after 9, 10, 12 years, "Boy, I can still do it." Look at the film and you really can't still do it as good as you used to do it. And your enthusiasm isn't there as much.

I knew it was all over. I had lost a lot of weight and my back was killing me. I couldn't run at all and what had been my trademark, my strength and quickness, was gone. A lot of it was mental, because I had a lot on my mind. I was going through my divorce. The night before we beat San Francisco 30-28 in that comeback in the NFC playoff game, we were playing poker. When I got out of the chair, I couldn't straighten up to go back to my room. I knew that night that was the end. We played the Redskins in the championship game and got killed 26-3. I played at 208 pounds. I talked to Tom about it and I said, "I don't think I can play anymore." He said, "Well, that's something you have to evaluate on your own. You didn't have a great year and we're going to bring along the other guys." There was no question in my mind. It was a fair evaluation by all parties. The fallacy that you have is the parade is going to continue for you. But someday you can come to the end of the parade route and the parade's over. You're no longer in it.

XII

Pain and Injury

Pain never bothered me. I missed one game in college. It was my junior year against Boston College. The week before, we were playing Syracuse and I got a severe hip pointer. The muscle on my hip slipped off. I was blocking Ernie Davis and my hip pad came down and he just fell on me. I had never had a hip pointer. I had never had anything that would keep me out. I thought I was indestructable, but I tell you, this hurt.

At halftime, I went in and told the doctor I could hardly breathe, but I was going to play the second half against these guys. I said, "What can you do?" He said, "I can block it." So I said, "Then block it." I got a couple shots of novocaine and played the second half. In those days, to say you wanted a shot of novocaine in college, they thought you were nuts.

I got through the game, but it didn't do a lot of good. I thought I was going to do yeoman service. We got beat 35-0. Syracuse was on its way to the national championship. I didn't have pain, but I didn't play worth a darn. The next day I could not get out of bed it hurt so bad. I missed the Boston College game. I had a big pot on my gut where it looked like all the muscles had fallen down. It was terrible. That was the first time I'd ever taken a shot. I never did it in college after that.

The next year, we were going to play Syracuse up there. I ran into a blocking sled in a Thursday night practice trying to catch a pass. I almost broke my hand, arm and everything else. But I played the whole game and we won 10-0.

I think I played with pain and I think most guys played with pain because they were afraid to come off the field for fear someone would take their job. I really believe this. It was kind of expected of you, part of the macho image, but I think you were afraid you were going to lose your job if you didn't play.

In the pros, taking shots became sort of a pattern. I took them and I saw other people do it. I saw Rick Casares do it, Bill George, Fred Williams. You had to stop and wonder what kind of guys these guys were that they would take shots to play football. If I said I really respect them for doing that, I'm sure some people would say I'm nuts. Well, I do respect them for doing that because they had a lot of pride in what they were doing. They had enough dedication to go out and try to do it when they weren't 100 percent. I'm not saying it's right or wrong. Maybe what Alex Karras said in that movie, *Against All Odds,* is right. Maybe we were all dumb for doing it that way.

But the only security you had back then was in playing and playing well. If you weren't playing, it meant somebody else was playing and your security blanket was taken away. I think all of us had a fear of that. There weren't that many jobs. There were only 36 guys on a team when I was a rookie with the Bears and only 12 teams.

The worst injury I ever had was my foot. I have a deformed foot because of it and it led to a degeneration of my hip. I have an artificial hip because of the foot injury. It happened before the 1965 season during a scrimmage against the College All-Stars. I caught a pass out of bounds and a guy fell on my right foot and it went flat. It was dislocated. I stood up and my arch cracked and went to the ground. They put it in a cast. It was fine for a while. About two weeks after they put it in a cast, I was bouncing around on it. We used to go down to a bar in Rensselaer and get into twist contests. That's really something to be up there twisting with a cast on your leg. Then one day, I was fooling around going through the ropes in practice with the cast still on and I heard something go pop. I'm not sure I didn't dislocate it again in the cast and that was the way it healed, because when they took off the cast, I told them no way, put it back on. I couldn't stand up on it. I couldn't put my foot on the accelerator or the brake of my car. I went home and soaked it and did everything they told me. Limp, limp, limp, limp. I couldn't put a shoe on, it hurt so bad, because there was so much calcium forming on top. Then they gave me one of those rigid steel-toed shoes. I missed the whole exhibition season, but when it came to the first league game, I started. I got it blocked with a shot before the game and got it blocked again with a shot at halftime. I played every game that year. But it took speed away from a guy who had no speed. It led to me walking different, running different, and led to a lot of problems.

They did what they thought was best for it. I saw a doctor recently and he told me there were three joints that were not in place, so it was a dislocation that was not set properly or else it was set properly and I loosened it in the cast. By the time they took the cast off, it had already formed that way, so there was nothing they could do. I started favoring it and getting pulled muscles. My back started hurting. Eventually, my hip started hurting. My hip really started hurting years after I got out of football and became a runner.

The year after I first hurt the foot, I had an operation on it. They cut the bone growth and all the calcium off. Then I went out and played golf on it and it got infected. So they had to cut again. This time, they let me watch the operation. They cut the infection out.

The hip was still not that big a problem when I came to Chicago to coach. I could still run. Halas had an artificial hip and he always took time out to talk to people about his operation. He was one of the pioneers in the process. My hip started deteriorating rapidly from arthritis in 1983. The ball was starting to crack and the socket had no cartilage left. It was bone rubbing on bone. It stopped me from bending over. If I could get my right leg up, I used to have to hook my sock over my toe because I couldn't bend that far. I made the decision to have total hip replacement shortly after Halas passed away. We used a new process called the fiber metal process. There is no glue or cement used. The bone grows naturally to the replacement. It's not perfect, but it's good. I have no pain in the hip. I have pain in the outside muscles of my leg and I still limp, but it's mostly because of the foot. I can run and the hip will get better and better and my leg will get stronger and stronger. There's a possibility I didn't give it enough time to heal. There's a rumor to that effect. I didn't make medical history. I played golf on it in six weeks. Waddled up to the tee with a cane, hit the ball, then waddled back to the cart with a cane and went on my way.

I probably could have a little bit of a case for filing an injury grievance against the Bears, but that's life. The only thing wrong with my foot is it didn't heal fast enough to get me out on the field when I wanted to be out on the field. It healed

crooked. That's life. I can't help it. Now, guys say, "I was released from the team when I had a pulled hamstring." Well,
tough shit. So what?

I thought there was something that said nobody ever
forces you to do anything. Nobody put a gun to any of these
guys' heads to play football. That's what makes me laugh. It
doesn't make me laugh; it makes me cry. Our society has become a sue society. Do a little, gain a lot. Break the big guy
down. Make the corporation pay. I always thought this country was based on going out and getting your fair share through
work and effort. If I get hurt, I get hurt. Maybe they'll pay my
hospital bills, which they should do, and I'll go back about my
business. Things have changed. I could never in all my
thoughts think about filing a workman's compensation claim
or anything against the league or the Bears. Every opportunity
I had came from football and I knew the risk when I went in.

I hear Moms today say, "I hope my kid is a good baseball
player because football is too tough." I say, "Hey, if you feel
that way, don't let him play." Be realistic. There are risks. There
are great risks right now in football, especially if you come up
in a program where they stress winning instead of teaching at a
young age. Then you have a problem. But I could never understand biting the hand that feeds you. It's a dog eat dog world
and everybody's got to eat.

I had other injuries. I hurt my knee my first year with the
Bears. You know who hurt it? Ted Karras missed a block and
hit me in the knee. Same guy I yelled at in my first game as a
rookie. Tore the inside ligaments. There were only two weeks
left in the season. I told the trainer, Ed Rozy, to tape it as hard
as he could on Saturday. I told Halas I thought I could go. We
played Cleveland and I caught seven passes. Played the whole
game. I played the last game against the Vikings, too. I was
voted to go to the Pro Bowl and Mr. Halas said he wasn't going
to let me go. I said, "You've got to let me go." It was $800 in

those days if you won. Halas sent me down to see a doctor in Baltimore. He looked at the knee and told me I had torn ligaments, but they had started healing. He said he couldn't do any better if he operated. He told me I would have a loose knee the rest of my life, but I would probably be O.K.

"Can I go to the Pro Bowl?" I asked.

"You tell Mr. Halas if he doesn't let you go to give you the money. He'll let you go," said the doctor.

He was exactly right.

In 1964, I dislocated my shoulder against the College All-Stars. I caught a pass and had my arm on the ground trying to keep my balance when someone hit me across the arm. The shoulder kept dislocating and I didn't play in one exhibition game. I played the whole year with a harness. That was the year I caught 75 passes. I could hardly lift the arm. We didn't have a good team. We threw the ball all the time.

In Dallas once, I was waiting to take one of the players home from a nightclub. Worse came to worse and we were leaving the place when it was closing time, which was wrong. I shouldn't have been there in the first place. Finally, my friend went home with somebody else and that left me to drive home by myself. I was fine, but I was really tired. As I was driving down the road, a guy and girl came roaring out of a blind apartment area onto the main road. There was no chance for me to stop. They were lucky I didn't kill them. I wasn't going that fast, only 45 or 50. I never really had a chance to slow down either. We hit with such force that the steering wheel bent and my mouth hit the top part of the steering wheel. It knocked my teeth back in my mouth and broke a bone. Plus, I pulled a muscle in my arm. All I wanted to do was get home and have the guy pay for the teeth.

I called Dan Reeves when I got home and told him I was in a car accident. He was a player-coach then. I told him I was O.K., but I wanted to see a dentist first thing in the morning. It was 1:30 a.m. He said he was going to come over. When he got there and saw me, he said, "Oh my God." He had already called a dentist. He got a dentist up and an oral surgeon and an orthodontist. It was the most amazing thing. Three of them worked on me until 4 or 4:30 in the morning. It was Friday morning.

I told them, "I'm playing Saturday night."

They said, "You can't play with these teeth."

I said. "Take 'em out."

They said they would wire the teeth in and build a brace. I told them no one was going to hit me in the mouth anyway.

He said, "You better hope not, because if they do, it's going to hurt."

He put them in and protected them with one of those big plastic things. I got my arm shot up and played.

Once in Philadelphia, I had a hamstring injury and shouldn't have played. But we were in Pittsburgh and my parents and brother were there. I got a shot during the game on the sidelines. Just pulled down the pants, had everybody stand around, and got the shot. It wasn't a great decision. I went back in and played, but I was very ineffective. I ran full blast into a goal post. They still show it in "Football Follies."

Today, there are more teams and more leagues. Players don't look at playing hurt the same way. Overall, it has changed to a more protective nature. I watch a lot of players who play it the way it's supposed to be played. I see players limping out there and playing as hard as they can on one leg. I see other guys who take it easy. Every individual is different. One person puts a certain value on sports and someone else doesn't put the same value on it. One says football is a means to an end; another says football is the end, because when they're done, they don't want to have to work. They look at the financial end of it.

When we played, it was a means to an end. We didn't

make a lot, but we always felt it could get you into things you could do later. You always heard of the football player who got a good education and became a salesman or got a car dealership. You never heard of an athlete who retired on his own with the money he had in the bank. But it has become this way because of the super salaries. Longevity comes to people's minds. Look at the severance pay. Players say, "Hey, if I don't do it this week, or for the next three or four weeks, maybe I can get another year out of it." As a former player, I find it very hard to believe anybody could think that way. I don't see how you can have very much commitment to what you're doing. The only way I look at it is if you have a chance to do something, do it. Do it the best you can and then if you can't get it done, walk away with your head up high and say you gave it your best shot. I'm sure there are people who think it's good to stick it to the organization, but I just don't understand that.

Sure, when I played, I saw some people who couldn't play hurt as well as others could. I saw a few guys who learned how to nurse a sprained ankle or a pulled muscle for weeks and months. Those guys never lasted long. They were on the outside looking in a year later. I think that's what you've got to be afraid of.

FROM LANDRY TO HALAS

XIII

Landry Calls Again

A group of us got involved in a singles bar operation after the Cowboys won their first Super Bowl and we really felt we were going to become very successful and very wealthy. We were thinking about going national and making a big deal out of it. But everybody was greedy and it didn't work out. When I retired, I was going to work in that business. It wasn't a week after I retired, I got another call out of the blue from Tom. He said, "Why don't you come and talk to me?" I knew he wasn't asking me out of retirement, because I saw the films. I knew how bad I was. He said, "Have you ever thought about coaching?" I said I had thought about it. "Do you want to take a shot at working with our receivers?" he asked.

I was ecstatic. I asked when he had to know. He told me to

take my time and give him a decision in the next week or so. I went to the restaurant and I thought about it and I looked at that place and I looked at the people in the place and I thought, "If I don't get out of here, I'm going to be standing up at that bar for the rest of my life." I picked up the phone and said, "I'd like to take that job."

My salary dropped from $44,000 as a player to $22,000 as a coach, but that was the best opportunity I ever had. Of all the people besides Halas, it would have to be Tom that I'd have to be grateful for. I have to look at it this way, though. I still think in life, even though people are important and provide opportunities, what the person does with the opportunities is what is important. My wife, Diana, recently asked me who I would thank if I had to thank somebody for where I'm at, not that I'm at anywhere. She asked, "If you had to thank one person, who would it be?" I said I would thank two people. I would thank God that I am who I am, that my parents were who they were, that I had the opportunities I had in life. Then I'd thank myself, because I did it. I don't care what else happened, whether it was good or bad, I still persevered enough to overcome problems and get to where I'm at. She was kind of surprised. She said, "Well, I thought you would have said Coach Halas or Coach Landry." She thought my answer was a little egotistical. And it wasn't. It's not meant to be that way. It's just that I believe that people are placed in your life for reasons. I really believe that very definitely.

Another thing is if you want things in life, wanting and wishing for things don't mean a crap. They just don't mean anything. I think if you really desire something or will something, things start happening. My coaching career was interesting the way it developed. I thought for a long time about coaching, then broadening out in coaching, then wanting to be coach of the Bears. I never said a word about it. Maybe I talked to Dan Reeves, but not very many people. Yet I thought about it. The first time I really thought about coming to the Bears was when Jack Pardee left after 1977. Bill Gleason of the Chicago Sun-Times called me about it and I said, "I'm not ready for that job." And I wasn't. But I said, "There will come a day when I will be."

I started out working with the receivers and then added special teams and ended up handling the passing game after Dan left in 1981 to become head coach in Denver. But Tom always kept a finger on it. He always put a few plays in that we wanted, but unless he really liked them, he wouldn't call them. There is a saying about everyone being pregnant with ideas. Fine, be pregnant with them. But be practical with them, too. When I first coached special teams, I'd tell Tom, "We can fake a punt. We can onside kick." He never let me do those things. We were successful with special teams for a number of years, but we never tried any spectacular plays. I did an onside kick in New York one year. We were playing the Giants in Shea Stadium and we had just scored. We never scored a lot on the Giants. I figured I'd tell Toni Fritsch to onside kick. I told him, "You tell them we'll go onside kick right. We'll recover it and they don't have a chance. Only thing is, just kick it far enough so in case we don't get it, they won't get it." Toni gave a wink. They lined up and I can still see it. He kicks it on the baseball infield and the dust is flying and the ball is bouncing and we should have it. But the ball goes out of bounds and we've got to kick it again. I was standing on the sidelines up by where the kickoff team was. Tom was down on the other side. He started toward me and I could see him coming. I kept moving until I couldn't move any farther. I got to the end of the coach's box and he walked up beside me. He was looking out on the field and he said between clenched teeth, "If you ever do that again without telling me, you'll be looking for a job." I got the point. That's exactly what he said. Without even looking at me. He was looking at the field the whole time.

I was put into Dallas for a reason, probably to learn a lot about myself through other people and probably Coach Landry more than anybody else. I would say I tested him pretty good as a player and as a coach.

My temper got me in trouble a few times. I don't think my temper was a problem when I was a player. I don't think anybody ever said anything about my temper. Tempers are nice when you're a player. A coach would like that. Why wouldn't he? Everybody talks about temper or anger, but what about somebody saying, "But what about his competitive nature?" Dan Reeves got angry, too, but it was because he competed. Lee Roy Jordan got mad, but it was because he competed. Bob Lilly used to get violent, but he competed. But when you take that temperament and put it into an assistant coach, or a head coach, and then you get angry, then you're no longer competing. Then you're becoming a hothead because you're not setting the example you should. I know that. As a player, you have an outlet. Temper has hurt a lot of coaches. I think you learn to control it from maturity. It doesn't come overnight. If I can last 10 more years, I'll be better 10 years from now than I am now. I'm better now than I was three years ago. I was better two years ago than I was nine years ago. I think you kind of mellow with age. There are some guys who have no reason to mellow. But I guarantee you Chuck Knox mellowed. Maybe Bill Walsh never had to mellow. Maybe Tom Landry never really had to mellow. I think probably Chuck Noll had to mellow. I don't know if Don Shula ever had to. They never make any bad calls against him anyway.

I had to learn to control my temper because Tom made that very apparent after I threw a couple clipboards. The worst time I really threw the clipboard was a Thanksgiving Day game on national television against Houston in 1979. We were winning the game and the Oilers were driving. I had the special teams and the Oilers got into the fringe area between a punt and field goal. I told both the field goal rush team and the punt return team to be ready. It turned out to be a punt, but an extra guy from the field goal rush team, Dave Stalls, went running out onto the field. I was screaming at the top of my voice to come back. It was incredible. He had to hear me unless he was stone deaf. Of course, nobody on our team took the time to count our players. They lined up and punted the ball and the flag went down. They got a first down and went in to score. They won the game 30-24. After the game, the reporters asked Tom what happened and he said to ask Mike. I wouldn't talk to anybody. I was really pissed. I mean the kid was totally wrong. He was a backup and the only reason he was on the team was because Randy White was hurt. It just infuriated me so badly. I didn't sleep at all that night. I had guys calling me to ask what happened. I said, "I'll take the blame, but if you can't understand the difference between field goal rush and punt return, we've all got problems." I wasn't afraid to take responsibility, but my goodness, it couldn't have been any clearer than I tried to make it on the sideline and here's a guy who goes off half-cocked. It just really killed me. We lost a football game on national TV because of a stupid-ass play. That's when I really threw the clipboard.

I threw a football in Pittsburgh once. One of the greatest shots I ever had in my life. Ron Johnson, one of the Steelers' cornerbacks, hit Drew Pearson out of bounds. It was a penalty, no question about it, but they didn't look like they were going to call anything. So as he hit him and nothing was called right away, the ball came rolling over by me. I picked it up left-handed and as they were walking back onto the field, I threw it left-handed and it hit Johnson in the back of the head. By that time, they had thrown a flag against Pittsburgh for a 15-yard penalty. Then they threw a 15-yard penalty on me. I apologized to Ron afterwards and told him it was a one in a million shot. I can't even throw left-handed, yet the ball went about 10 yards and it just dinked him in the back of the helmet. Kind of amazing. But that was a silly thing to do, just a stupid-ass thing to do. Why would I want to do that? But I was so frustrated. I never got more frustrated than when we played Pittsburgh, because they had our number. I used to tell Dan Reeves, "I think it's the black jerseys. When they put those black jerseys on we go into a shell." I really thought that. They used to let us beat them in the exhibition season and then kick our butts in the regular season.

I threw a clipboard down once against Pittsburgh in an exhibition game and Tom took me to the woodshed on that one. He said something on the field quietly. He would just walk up and talk, but he would be fuming. He called me in the next day and said, "I just can't have that happen. If it happens again, I'm going to let you go."

I don't think Landry knows what he looks like on the sideline. That's him. On the sideline, he is totally engrossed in what he is doing. I've heard him say things. He gets mad, too, but what the heck, when you have a reputation as a guy who gets mad, the camera is on you more than it's on the game. In the case of him, it's never on him, so he doesn't have to worry. He's so engrossed in the game, he doesn't know whether he's laughing or smiling or not. Tom was probably the epitome of a man at peace and in the job he had it wasn't always easy to be that. There was a lot of turmoil when I played for him. A lot of things will make a coach crazy—the wrong article in the newspaper, the wrong thing said by a player. A lot of things can throw you off guard. Tom is very active in the Fellowship of Christian Athletes and he does great justice to it in his life. He is sincere. What you see is what you get. You don't get what you don't see and you don't see what you don't get. He is what he is. When he says the most important thing to him is his God, his family, and his job, and he lives his life that way, then that's pretty darn good. A lot of people can say that, but if I start wondering where a buck is coming from instead of where my spiritual life is, then I have a problem. My priorities can get mixed up. I don't think he ever gets his priorities mixed up.

I don't force my religion or my beliefs on anybody, but there is no way I would be here without them. I always had faith, but I never had understanding. I always knew what was going on in life. I was raised right. I served as an altar boy in the Catholic church. I did all the things you were supposed to do. But I never understood why I was supposed to do them, because I never had a total understanding of what was going on. The underlying thing wasn't there. I went through life believing that you did certain things, you lived by certain rules, and society accepted them as being right. I'm far from perfect now and I'm never going to be perfect. When I die, I'm going to be still trying to get better than I am. In 1977, I was a guy who had a lot going for me. I was doing what I wanted to do. Everything was going pretty good. I was making enough money, driving a nice car. I had a good family and a nice home. But I was very unhappy and I kept trying to figure out why I was so unhappy. It was basically that I had no spiritual life at all.

It was like a constant turmoil inside. I couldn't figure out why I didn't have the same feelings other people had. I saw people around me who seemed to be at peace with themselves and I could never get at peace with myself. I was always struggling from within. Then a couple of the coaches, Jerry Tubbs and Bob Ward, invited me to a Bible study with some of the players. What I saw and what I heard and what I understood really made a big impact on me. I just felt that I had lived too much of my life selfishly.

As a kid, you grow up and say, "I want to do that and this, and want to be this and that." There's a "me" syndrome in our society of setting goals. That's not wrong, because if you don't set goals you won't make it. But if it's solely you and your goals, then you start believing you're the beginning, the means, and the end of all this stuff. That's what I was believing and it wasn't working. I knew there was something more important. When I started attending these Bible studies, I really did have a great feeling. I understood completely that my part in this whole thing was so small it didn't really matter. I did have a part. The responsibility of executing this life to the best of my ability was given to me. It didn't matter what anybody else around was doing. I had to live to the best of my ability. I had a free will to choose right, wrong, up, down, and anything else I wanted to do. I started understanding that a heck of a lot better. Once I did, my life took a better direction. I was able to share my life with people better, to love people more, to take the time to try to understand their point of view a whole lot more. I became a better guy to work with and work for. I became a better employee, because I really had a lot more compassion for people and could understand people and their problems better.

The experience even helped curb my temper for a while. I'm not saying I was perfect. I would swear at times, but I don't think that's what it is all about. The Lord isn't out there making check marks when you swear or kick the sideline marker or throw a clipboard. The thing I'm saying is it's what you do in life for others and share with others. It's the feeling you have for people. If you read the Bible, the Good Lord had a temper, too. Threw a few people around. We all have it, but how do you use it? When do you control anger? Those are the things that become very important. I don't think I would have ever had the true direction in my life if it hadn't been for those changes. I was having success in my life, but if success could bring you that much unhappiness, then I couldn't take any more success, because I wasn't really enjoying it. There was an emptiness. Victories didn't mean a whole lot and I just couldn't get real close to people. Nothing was making me happy.

Then my life changed like night and day. My feelings inside still haven't changed. I get a little down on myself now and then, because I feel if I really believed all this, I would be setting a good example all the time. I can't do it. I can't be the right example all the time. I wish I could but I can't. And I don't need some preacher to come and tell me what the right example is. I know in my heart what's right and what's wrong. I know when I do something wrong. Nobody has to tell me. Inherently, man knows right from wrong. Anybody who says he doesn't, that's wrong. You know right from wrong even as a baby before anybody ever told you. When I do something wrong, it bothers me. Maybe wisdom is saved for the old and as I get older, I'll get smarter. Maybe I'll make more right decisions and do less wrong things. I had a good upbringing in Catholic grade school and my mom was a very devout Catholic. I went to mass all the time and served on the altar until I was almost a senior in college. That was a good thing. That really gave me some stability through the early years. Then I guess I kind of lost it in pro ball when you think you're the source of all power, the beginning and the end.

There is a lot of confusion about the role of religion in sports. Sometimes you hear players or coaches talk about God's will affecting wins and losses. That's a fallacy. The scripture tells us we are given earthly talents of body and soul and mind to do the best we can. Our total belief as Christians is to lead our lives in such a way as to spend eternity with our maker. All religions are based on that philosophy. The Christian religion is based on the Son of God and the Trinity and the whole evolution of how that came about and why it's a fact and why He will come again in the end, which I believe totally. But I believe that any person who doesn't take the talents he is given or takes them and misuses them is really being a hypocrite in every form, worse than people who are hypocrites in other ways. I think the worst thing you can do is have a talent and not use it. The reason I say that is everybody is not created equal. It says that, but it isn't true. We're not. In the eyes of God, we're all created equal, but physically, we are not all created equal. You see kids in hospitals, kids who are crippled, mentally ill. When you have a talent, a God-given talent of health and intelligence in body and strength and speed, and then you lose a game and say it's God's will, I don't agree. I don't believe God wills you to lose. I believe God wills you to do the best you can at whatever you are doing. If you're painting a building, paint it the best you can. If you're playing football, baseball, hockey, do it the best you can. If you write a bad story, you write a bad story. It wasn't God's will. It was me. I wrote a bad story. I missed the tackle. I dropped the ball. It was me. You know why? My concentration was bad. You know why? My mind's somewhere else. Maybe I was thinking it wasn't that important. If people say it's God's will, maybe I'm missing the boat.

XIV

Maturing As a Coach

I think Tom wanted me to be sort of a link between the coaches and players. I know he didn't want me for my coaching prowess. Dan Reeves had left the staff for that 1973 season to go into business. I think Tom wanted to know what players were thinking. He had been accused of not being close to them and he wanted someone to be a sounding board. I talked to them.

It's a very hard thing to come out as a coach with the same team. I became more effective when a lot of those guys I played with were gone. I had to tell Billy Truax he couldn't carry 250 pounds on a bad knee. He was a good friend and I was talking to him as a friend. I wasn't trying to impress anybody with any great coaching knowledge. We knew what we had to do assignment-wise. We could either do it with a little force and excitement or we could just go through the motions. The best thing we did down there is we got excited about ourselves for a while and played really super football.

My early coaching days were a maturing process. As a player, you don't understand that things have to be done in a certain way and in a certain order. You think that seems kind of childish. Yet that's the procedure that has to be followed. As a player, you really don't want to be bothered with details. And that's what the coaches emphasized. As a player, you think the most important thing is the game on Sunday. You don't really understand all those things that lead up to playing the game the way it's supposed to be played—the practices, the meetings, the discipline. In coaching, you find out if you don't do the little things, you're not going to do the big things either. It's repetitious and boring. One thing I learned as a coach from Coach Landry was it is foolish to assume a player knows anything from one year to the next. You start from scratch. Then, as soon as you say, "Slant 24," they say, "Oh yeah, we know slant 24."

"Do you know what you do on your adjustment against this defense?"

"Well, let's see, Oh yeah, I remember that."

They remember what they see. Tom always showed you how to do things even when he wasn't capable of showing you how to do things. Halas did it, too. Tom would get down and say, "This is the way I want you to do it." Some of the things were funny because his knee would bother him and his back was bothering him. But he would get down and do his best to show it. It's one thing to do everything on the blackboard, but when you get out with the players, you better get in and show them what you're talking about. If I can demonstrate a block to the tight ends, how to hit the machine and drive it, it will be easier for the player to understand.

Jean Fugett, a tight end who came to Dallas in my last year, accused me in *Sports Illustrated* of teaching dirty tactics. Jean didn't know how to block, so I don't know how he could accuse anybody of hitting anybody dirty or clean. He thought any time you made contact it was illegal. We teach that when you come out to block, you close your fists and come up with your hands underneath the guy's solar plexus and hit him in the stomach. It stops you from getting your hands out where you're holding and it helps you deliver a blow as you come up on him. Nothing illegal about it. You couldn't hurt a guy in a hundred years. Fugett said I told them to hit them in the groin. I never said that. That's probably been done, even though it's not within the rules. I just said to bring them up and hit the guy in the solar plexus. Where are you going to put your hands when you're blocking? On your hips? Anybody who thinks it isn't legal, they ought to put a dress on and get out on the football field. But even though it's all within the rules, I can't find too many guys who will close their fists and do it because football has come to a pushing game with the hands extended. I don't think it should be that way. We spend a lot of money for helmets and shoulder pads. Heck, we ought to put big pads on our hands to block with. Doesn't make sense to me.

When I went into coaching, I had been a player all those years and I thought I knew a lot. I thought I had a lot of knowledge about defenses and how to run routes and all that. I knew nothing. I really didn't have an understanding of why defenses were playing a certain way. As a tight end, I had studied only linebackers and safeties. I never understood the whole defense. As a coach, it was completely different. In the beginning it was kind of tedious to learn all those things, but you had to learn them because you had to teach them.

Another thing players don't understand is why you have a curfew. I'm not even sure I understand it now. It seems foolish to me that they wouldn't want to come in. As a player, I always thought the same thing—if I wasn't going to come in, I wasn't going to come in regardless of whether I was being fined or not. You understand now that our game has changed to the point that if a player were to abuse curfew the night before a game, he's really jeopardizing his career, the outcome of the game, the welfare of his teammates. There are so many things involved. In the olden days, it was really no different. Nobody should ever abuse curfew, but my goodness, some of the guys who used to never come in for curfew were some of the best players on the field. As a coach, you had to make allowances, I guess.

Without question, the most influential part of my life was the Dallas experience for 13 years. I learned nearly all my football there. The impression the Cowboys gave an outsider was they were a finesse team that didn't get down in the trenches with you. Then you found out differently. There is no such thing in football as a strictly finesse team. You can only finesse so long and then you have to put on the boxing gloves and go out there. They had a subtle way. They could knock you out with a lot of different punches, but they still could stay in close and fight with you. I never knew that as an opponent. I was just never a Cowboy fan. The more I got to know Tom, I think maybe that is the image he would like to portray. I'm not sure he wouldn't rather get right in there and knock your block off—rush the ball 350 yards down your throat. It's like Washington. Joe Gibbs would like you to think he is moving people around and throwing the ball all over the place. All of a sudden you look at the final stats and John Riggins ran for 144 yards. Bill Walsh in San Francisco uses the pass to set up the run, but when you look at it, the 49ers rush the ball for 200 yards.

I have more of a ball-control philosophy than Tom had. The only bad thing is if you don't score points in a ball-control offense, you have a problem. I believe ball-control eliminates a lot of negatives. It keeps the defense off the field and keeps you out of critical kicking situations. Tom is going to strike you a little quicker. There was a time when it seemed like the Cowboys scored a touchdown on the first series every game. He uses play-action passes very well and I believe the primary part of the passing game is play-action. That's another thing I learned from him. We won the Super Bowl on play-action passes.

I don't think there's any one way to win. You have to be flexible. Ball control can mean different things. First downs are more important than time off the clock because they correlate to points scored. Time off the clock doesn't necessarily correlate to points, which we proved in 1984. You have to minimize your mistakes. Every once in a while you get a game when the score is 50-40 and both teams are throwing like crazy. To me, that's not football. I still think you win with defense and the most important thing is to develop your offensive line. I don't care how well you play defense, if you have no offensive line you have nothing because you can't protect the quarterback, you can't have a running game, and you can't do anything to complement the defense.

John Madden said he used to argue with Al Davis about what was more important. Madden said offensive line and Davis said cornerbacks. I think you're really pulling teeth with that. There's an old saying in baseball that your strength lies up the middle—your catcher, pitcher, shortstop, second, and center field. I'm not sure that's not true in football. Look at us up the middle out of an I-formation—Payton, Suhey, McMahon, Jay Hilgenberg at center, Singletary, Gary Fencik at free safety. We're pretty strong. But I think what Madden says is true. The offensive line is so important. I know the position that is so hard to find is cornerback. You're looking for the exceptional athlete who can run, cover, move his feet, has good speed to catch up, and is tough. If you can find them, you better keep them. It's harder to coach the offensive line. It's the hardest position to coach. Jim Myers has done a great job for so many years in Dallas and we have a guy, Dick Stanfel, who is just like Jim. They're like mother hens. They protect their players. They have to relate to them completely differently than a head coach does. They handle a group of five who are all different and they have to coach three different positions. To make that all work and blend together is really tough. But the offensive line is what it's all about. You don't do anything on offense without the line, period. I don't care who you are.

Tom encouraged discussions and arguments over strategy. When you stood up to defend your side, whether it be offense or defense or the kicking game, you better have the facts and be ready to back them up because somebody was going to try to punch a hole in it. The coaches in Dallas were always arguing about what's more important: when you do something or what you do. They usually agreed it was when you did something. I disagreed. I believed it was what you do. "When" you do the wrong thing doesn't mean beans. The key word I always fought for down there was "execute." It didn't matter what we were talking about or teaching as coaches unless we could execute. Tom would say, "Well, you're too basic." I would say, "No, I believe in all the things you're saying if they can understand it and execute it. But if they can't, then we have to go back to something we can do."

The Shotgun formation, or the Dallas "Spread", developed after some long conversations with Tom, Dan and me. Ed Hughes was there, too. Tom was talking about concepts of nickel defenses and blitzes. I said, "What if you put the quarterback away from the center, just like San Francisco did in the early 60s, and then move the backs up?" Then you could put the backs in motion and tell who was covering and who was in position to blitz. I think Tom had it in his mind to go that way anyway, so he asked us to draw up some formations and we did.

You hear a lot about the smooth Dallas "organization."
The people are outstanding. Not everything is peaches and
cream. It can't be, but the thing that was so impressive about
the Cowboys was I really felt everybody was geared to one
thing and that was winning. They gear their whole environment toward winning. They were not the highest-paid team in
football, yet they managed to come up with great leaders like
Roger Staubach and Randy White. They always had great
players like Bob Lilly, Dan Reeves, Walt Garrison, Lee Roy
Jordan, Cornell Green, Jethro Pugh. To take that many guys
with that much ability and to keep playing as a team for as
long as they did, that has to say something about the guy who
is running them, Tom Landry.

They all do a great job down there, but in every organization there is glue that holds the whole puzzle together. I think
he's the glue in what makes the whole thing flow and work.
He's a great buffer between players and management and players and assistant coaches. He controls it with an iron hand. I
don't think that has ever changed. He knows what's going on
all the time. Even during the trying times when I was playing,
he was a stabilizing factor in all the elements that were there.
For a time, he had the ability to keep things in-house and nothing got out to the newspapers. But they did eventually. Then
some books were written and things were said and a lot of the
Cowboys' image that was a silver badge got a little bit tar-
nished. You found out guys drink on the airplane after a game.
Of course, everything gets out now. You can't keep anything in.

Dallas got a lot of publicity for being a computerized
team. Every team has computers. They speed up the process of
sorting out tendencies. But assistant coaches still have to take
plays off film to feed to the computer. This is tedious and part
of the reason a coach's life is far from all glamorous. Some of
our coaches come in on Sunday nights after a game to start
grading film. They want to have the last week's game out of

their minds by the time they start work Monday morning on a new opponent. I usually come in early Monday morning, around 4 a.m., so I can get film done by 6 a.m. I look at our offensive film and concentrate on the point of attack; that is, where the ball is run through the line of scrimmage. Other coaches have to grade every pass route and every block or every fake. Grading is a subjective thing. I feel three out of four plays have to be made to play around championship level. If a tight end or wide receiver does the right thing on three out of four plays, you have a chance to win at a championship level. I found out that guys who graded out in the 50s and 60s never made it. Guys who graded out in the 70s, 80s, and 90s often did make it. But it's also true that some guys who graded out 85 percent didn't play very well.

When I get done watching film of Sunday's game, I will start on the next opponent until the rest of the coaches are done grading. Then we'll discuss what I saw, what they saw, and we'll agree or disagree on how the players played. We meet with the players and critique the film. We start out with the whole team watching the kicking game, then we split into groups of offense and defense. I'm with the offense. There have been times when we will watch the whole film as a team, but that's just to let everybody see who is doing what. Most of the time, we split up.

The players go through a light running period on Mondays to work out the kinks and then they lift weights. They go home and the coaches go to work.

We watch film of the upcoming opponent and formulate ideas for the game plan. I usually stay in my office on Monday night, but I don't watch film all night. When I'm in the office at 4 a.m., I'm on the couch asleep. I don't fool anybody with that crap. By staying, it gives me an early start on Tuesday in case I want to work out before I start watching film again. Usually, I'll run up and down the halls. We watch film until about noon, sometimes later depending on the opponent. Then the defense comes together as a staff and the offense comes together as a staff to formulate our game plans.

Basically, a game plan is your plan of attack against what you expect the other team to do. Not all of the offensive or defensive plays in your repertoire will work well against every team. You want to emphasize the ones that will work. Tuesdays are pretty long. The players have the day off, but not the coaches. On offense, we put together the runs and the play-action passes and what we call deceptives. Every coach has his own ideas of which plays will work. Sometimes the game plan gets too long.

By Wednesday, every player has a copy of the game plan when he arrives. We meet and go over it, break for lunch, and then go to the practice field, where we concentrate mainly on the running game. After the Wednesday practice, the coaches watch film of the practice to see how each player is doing his job. We plan for the Thursday practice and put in more of the passing game. I tape my television show on Wednesday night.

What we tried to do in 1985 was change looks and formations more than change plays. We ran the same plays with different looks. That helped us a lot because there are only so many things you can do. The more things you put in, the more they have to learn and the less time we have to teach it.

Every coach has his ideas of what's right and what's wrong. We all try to copy the other people too much when we see them have success. George Allen did a good job of copying. He ran the same plays the Bears ran in the 60s. Football is football. You can put your priority on confusing people or you can put your priority on execution. I like to move people, but I still put the priority on execution. All the rest is icing on the cake. Do you think Chuck Knox cares if they call him Ground Chuck? Chuck Noll is another one. Coach Landry is another one. Their passing games are fairly basic. They're not as involved as a San Diego. And how much more basic can you be than the Raiders? Yet they still have a great passing game because they're not afraid to strike you off play-action for the big pass. For years in Chicago, they didn't use as many of the tools that they had here. And maybe they used one or two tools too much. They thought for a time the only guy who could run the ball was Walter and the only guy who could catch it was James Scott. That's where you make a mistake. We have a lot of guys who can run and a lot who can catch. We try to use them all. I know that makes some players mad, but I can't worry about that. Players get offended and think they're not as important. They are as important, but they're important to the team, not to their contract or to their incentive clauses. I'd like to see more contracts with team incentives. If we win 13 games, players get $20,000 more, or something like that.

On Thursdays, we practice more running and add the third-down passing plays. On Thursday night, we put in short-yardage plays, goal-line plays, our two-minute drill, and our "plus-territory" plays inside the 20. We practice those on Friday. Some teams practice offense one day and defense the next. We practice both every day. Some defensive coaches might not agree, but we've given the defense in Chicago as much time as we take on offense, except maybe for five minutes a day. That's really unheard of in most places. The defense felt they needed the time and we gave it to them. I never objected because what's good for the team is what's important. That would be the biggest difference between Chicago and the way Tom does it in Dallas. There, the offense got much more time on the field than the defense. After doing it the way we've done it, I wouldn't change it. We might take an extra 10 minutes on offense and do something with the running game, because it's that important.

It shouldn't take more time to learn offense than defense

the way defense is played today. I don't know that offense is any harder than defense.

On Saturday, we have a light workout in the morning and concentrate on special teams. On Saturday afternoon we either fly to our game or report to our hotel in Chicago to get ready for Sunday's game. You can see why games on Monday night or Thursday night or Saturday afternoon disrupt our schedule so much.

XV

Halas Answers My Letter—'82

The disagreements between Halas and me were blown out of proportion, but I'm sure there was some uneasiness there after I left. After I got to Dallas, I told him I wanted to come back and finish my playing career with the Bears. He said if I became a free agent, maybe something could be worked out. But it didn't happen. Then I saw him at a birthday party in the mid-70s. He asked me how I was doing in coaching. I said fine and he said I was doing a good job. It was a very good conversation.

In 1977, the Cowboys played the Bears in the first round of the playoffs. I feared that game, but we beat them handily 37-7. I don't know that I ever said, "Hey, I really wish I were on the other side of the field coaching those guys," but I think subconsciously that feeling was always there. When Jack Pardee left after that game, I didn't think I was ready. Jim Finks, general manager of the Bears, hired Neill Armstrong. I wasn't sure I could handle the total responsibility. It wasn't knowledge of the game; it was how you handle people and relate to people. That's not perfect now and won't be if I coach for 25 years, but in 1977, I didn't feel I was ready. The next year, my parents asked me what would make me happy and I said I wanted to be coach of the Bears.

I thought about it for three years. That was the only interest I had in head coaching. In 1981, I wrote Halas a letter. It was a simple letter. I just said I wanted to renew our friendship. I told him I knew he had experienced some troubled times. I said, "I just want you to know if you ever make a change in the coaching end of the organization, I just wish you would give me some consideration." That's all. It was a very nice letter.

I didn't hear from him until I got the phone call after the season telling me to come into Chicago. We did the deal right at his kitchen table. He liked that I went to bat for myself. My contract for $100,000 was by far the smallest in the league, but that's O.K. That wasn't my worry. My problem was whether I could get the job done. I wanted to prove to Mr. Halas that he made the right decision.

Nobody else in the National Football League would have hired me, no question. Too many drawbacks. There's an NFL image you have to be and maintain and I probably wasn't it. They want someone who can say all the right things to the media. Owners also want coaches who have a track record. Bud Grant said it proved it's not what you know; it's who you know. I'm just glad Halas knew me. Bud forgot he had to know somebody to get hired, too, a guy named Finks when he was in Minnesota. I have great respect for Bud Grant. I say a lot of things I wish I could take back. What he said hurt me at that moment, but he was hurt, too. Neill was his buddy, his friend, and he had a right to say it.

A lot of people said I'd never be a head coach. They say that about a lot of people. But I was given the opportunity. The key to success in life is opportunity and what you do with it. I called up Foge Fazio. I had played with him at Pitt and he had just been named head coach at Pitt. I said, "It could only happen in America. A Ukie and an Italian get a job on the same day. We're supposed to be working in the steel mills somewhere and here we are coaching football." We talked about it and laughed about it. I really believe that's what makes this country great.

Halas told me, "You are responsible to only one person: me. You don't have to answer to anybody else ever. You run the football team; I won't bother you. If I see something I disagree with, I'll tell you."

There was no conversation about the past.

He hired me for two reasons: first, he wanted to hire his guy, not someone somebody else hired. Second, he believed I'd be tough enough not to take any b.s. from anyone.

He said, "I would appreciate you talking to me once a week or so. Let me know your thinking and what's going on." We talked a couple times a week up until he got real sick in 1983. What he always wanted to know was what the attitude of the players was. He would ask, "How did practice go? Were they good practices? Did they drag?" I would tell him when we had good ones and when we had bad ones. Those are the things he wanted to know.

The only time he really said anything after a game was after we didn't score near the goal line in our first game against Detroit in 1982. He said, "You should have quarterback sneaked it." He sent the drawings of how to run a quarterback sneak against an even-man line and an odd-man line. I told Dick Stanfel regardless of whatever game we ever go into as long as I'm coaching here the quarterback sneak will be in the game plan in short yardage and goal line. I said we would learn to run it and run it well. How many times have we run the quarterback sneak and made it? We run it a lot. I still have the drawings.

He never called plays for me and I don't think for anybody else. The only other advice he gave me was to screw the reporters. He said, "You don't have to talk to them that much." I said, "Tell your grandson that." Pat McCaskey was the public relations man. Halas said "Well, when you go down there, you don't have to say anything."

I wasn't Jim Finks' guy, but I think he gave me the help I needed in certain areas. He didn't create tension. I felt I got along pretty good with Jim. But the only guy I was told I had to answer to was Mr. Halas. Every coach has to have full authority on the football end of it. If he gets too much intervention from owners or general managers, he's probably going to have problems somewhere along the line. That's one thing Tom Landry told me when I took the job. He said, "When you want to do it your way, make sure you do it your way. Because in the end, if you compromise and do it somebody else's way and it doesn't work, you'll kick yourself and say 'Gee, I wish I would have done it my way.' If you do it your way and it doesn't work, you have nobody to blame but yourself."

It was unusual that a coach would have his defensive staff already hired, but that was no problem. What made the situation bad the first year was myself and expecting too much with what we had. We didn't have enough to win. I thought we did. I fooled myself. We had nice guys, people who had played hard for the Bears. That's fine. I'll always respect them for that. But they weren't good enough to win championships with. Changes had to be made. If people don't have talent, that's fine. Just go out and break your ass and play as hard as you can. We had a lot of guys who did that. We had a lot of guys who didn't do that, too. We had a lot of guys who didn't have talent and didn't break their ass.

At our first minicamp in Phoenix, I said I wanted to go to the Super Bowl. Some of them had never heard that before. I did a lot of things. I told them to turn around to the guy behind them and say, "I love you." You should have seen the eyeballs roll then. If you never have been to the mountain, it's hard to understand what the mountain is like. Part of the problem in Chicago is that complacency set in. It almost seemed like the goal was to be average. The goal was never to be the best. People were always saying, "We can't compete with Minnesota or Detroit or Tampa Bay." It was a defeatist attitude. I thought we could be as good as anybody. We drafted well and had good people.

Rickey Watts missed the first day of our second minicamp and I cleaned out his locker. It could have been anybody. I wasn't trying to make an example out of Rickey. I did it basically to show he couldn't do what he wanted, that he had to work within the system, and he just wasn't that important. Nobody is that important. He had been around and never really fulfilled any of the great expectations they had for him. I just wanted to show who was boss and if anybody pulled those tricks, it would go the same way.

I don't know if I feel that way now. The way I look at it now, if a guy said he was going to miss, I'd fine him. But the first thing I would think is "Gees, I have to wonder about this guy on the field." If you're playing golf or tennis or boxing, fine. But you just happen to be playing a team sport and I think it's important you be around the team and share with the team. There's a camaraderie, a love, a feeling. You share your part of the responsibility by showing up and practicing. Nobody said it was fun, but everybody does it and it has to be done. I would probably fine the guy; I don't know if I'd clean out his locker.

The Bears made a great mistake bringing James Scott back from Canada right after I was hired. They felt to make Vince Evans effective at quarterback, they had to have Scott. Somebody sold Mr. Halas a bill of goods and they brought him back with guaranteed salaries and things. Scott wasn't the answer. I'm not taking anything away from what he contributed when he played. But he was 31, no legs left, out of shape. There was no way to justify it with his teammates who went out and played hard for a third of what he was making.

In a way, I felt sorry for Watts and Scott, though. We had to eliminate this crap in practice where the defensive backs were knocking the receivers apart. Our guys got hit harder in practice than they did in a game. Hey, that's your teammate. We had to play with those receivers. It would be like the receivers running live crackback blocks and cutting people. What are you going to achieve? I saw a linebacker take a tight end's head off in a dummy drill, which really made me mad. But what pissed me off more was the tight end didn't take the guy on right there and fight him. That tight end is no longer here. Regardless if you get your ass beat, you've got to take the guy on right there and establish yourself. "Hey, you're gonna play that way? I'm gonna play that way." Or, if you don't fight him right there, then the next time off the line you have to try to kill him. Even though it's your teammate. Because if you don't have your teammate's respect, you're never going to have your opponent's respect. We went through a period here where the defense just quit respecting the offensive players. But now look at our two backs, Suhey and Payton. Look at McKinnon as a blocker. Look at our offensive line. Those guys will take you on and they'll bite you. And the quarterback, too. McMahon will bite anybody.

Our first game in Detroit in 1982 still makes me mad. We lost 17-10 and if we would have won that game, I really believe 1982 would have been different. Instead of 3-6, we might have been 6-3. I think it happens for a reason. We couldn't even get in the right formation in Detroit. We had two guys off the line and nobody on the line, then two on the line and nobody off. It was a joke. It was our fault, not the players' fault. I thought there was no question about what we were doing. Evidently, there were a couple routes and things that sounded so much alike we caused some people to short circuit. I tell our coaches all the time, it doesn't matter how much I know or how much they know, the players have to play. It takes time to do the things you want to do. We might have been out there all day just trying to line up. I don't want to hear about that Detroit game ever again. Damndest thing I'd ever seen. We call a screen pass to the right, Walter runs for a touchdown, and we get our left tackle called for holding. Lazy Dan Jiggetts. Then he says, "Don't get mad." Don't get mad, my ass. It's my job. It's the difference between the Bears winning and losing.

When we lost our second game 10-0 to New Orleans, I think the players probably said, "This guy's crazy." I was never so humiliated. That was the day before the strike. Bum Phillips, the Saints' coach, asked me before the game, "Did your guy come over and ask our guy if they didn't want to play the game?" I said, "Gee, I don't think so, Bum. We know you're good, but we're not scared of you. At least I hope we're not." I'm not sure it didn't happen. That's when the captains were going back and forth, talking to each other, saying they were going to have a show of solidarity and there was going to be an eclipse in the east and the sun was going to rise in the west. I didn't know what the hell was going on with those people. I swore at them at halftime. I can understand getting beat and I can accept that. But that was a lethargic exhibition of football. We looked like we were dead-ass tired. We looked like we didn't want to play, like we didn't want to attack people. That was not the Bears' way of doing things. Our offensive line couldn't move anybody. Seven blocks of granite. Matt and Walter couldn't get to the line of scrimmage with basic football plays. I wasn't too nice. I did curse a lot and jumped and ranted and raved and told them they were cowards for not hitting anybody. Then I threw the chalk at the chalkboard. I'm sure they had seen nothing like that with the other people they had played for in their life. Ever. They got the message all right. They went on strike. They left a message for me: we're going to get rid of this S.O.B. for eight weeks. We won't have to put up with him anymore.

But after the strike ended, we went with McMahon and won three games and could have won more. We lost to Seattle 20-14 on a quarterback draw and a quick kick. I said we got beat by a team that shouldn't have beaten us and we got beat on a high school play. Their coach, Mike McCormack, said I insulted his team and showed my ignorance. I called and apologized. I didn't really mean to say it the way it came out. I respected Mike. It was a high school play, but it worked, so it was a hell of a play. I told him I wished he would have called me before he reacted.

The maddest I got the whole year was the last game in Tampa Bay. We lost in overtime 26-23 after blowing a 20-6 halftime lead. We made a change at halftime and I put in a play for short yardage and we didn't understand it. It backfired in a critical third down and one situation. We had two guys run the wrong way. If we had won the Tampa Bay game, we would have been in the playoffs our first year. I don't care if our record would have been 4-5. I don't care if we walk in, back in, or crawl in. We were in. The playoffs would have been interesting because as the scenario broke, we probably would have ended up playing Washington. I still think we would have matched up well against the Redskins. Of course, they won the Super Bowl.

HEAD COACH

XVI

I've Got to Relax—'83

I remember the losses. As a coach, you expect to win. When you lose, that's why you remember. I thought we were good enough to be in the 10-6 or 11-5 area in 1983. But we lost the opener to Atlanta and then blew overtime games to the Saints and Colts in the third and fourth weeks. Pretty soon we were 2-5.

Against Atlanta, Matt Suhey ran outside the hole on a critical play. We told him he would have made it if he had stayed inside. Against New Orleans, Suhey and Payton ran into each other in a critical situation and Vince Evans missed the handoff. We just weren't confident enough to do things under real pressure.

We went to Baltimore and I broke my hand after the

game. It became funny in a hurry, but it wasn't funny when it happened. We lost 22-19. What went through my mind is I was going to make this one point, really emphasize it. I saw a trunk and I thought, "I'm going to hit that thing for emphasis." And I really hit it. It broke. God damn, it hurt. I said, "Ooooh." I almost started laughing myself, but it hurt too much. I said, "Vince, say the Lord's Prayer. Doc, let's go."

I threw a headset in that game, too. Tried to kick it over the goal post. We just weren't doing the things we practiced all week, plus our game plan was too confusing. Too many runs in the game plan. We couldn't even practice all of them. I yanked Jimbo Covert out of the game. He was getting beat. He got beat because I didn't think he was working at it. Johnie Cooks was beating him. If he had beaten me that quick, he would have pissed me off so much I would have looked at it as a personal affront. I would have spent the whole day trying to kick his butt. I think his quickness surprised Jim so much he kind of lost his confidence. I think Dick Stanfel reminded me that it was only Covert's fourth game as a pro. I just wasn't listening. But I don't look at it that way. When I drafted Covert, I didn't look at him as being a rookie. He came in and played. In the first game he lined up, he was better than three-quarters of the tackles in the league.

Before the next game, I stood up with the cast on my right hand and said, "Win this one for Lefty." They liked that. I think they found out that this guy, he's not all right, but he's not all nuts either. We beat the Broncos 31-14, but the next week we had five turnovers and lost to the Vikings. That's when I got on Ken Margerum's butt for dropping a pass in front of the bench. Willie Gault fumbled a ball going into the end zone. I yanked McMahon. Evans fumbled. I got mad at the officials. The following week I said I had to relax. The worst thing about it is I wasn't taking those losses as Bear losses as much as I was taking them as my losses. If you put that much pressure on yourself, you're going to have a lot of problems. I was trying so hard to justify Mr. Halas's decision, to prove to everybody that it was the right choice, that we could win, that the things we were doing were the right things, that the way we were coaching was the right way.

McMahon and Evans and Margerum and some of the others said I was making them too tense, that they were too tight to make big plays. Anything can be a factor if you want it to be a factor. It can also be a copout. I didn't go out and throw the interceptions. I didn't misread the defense. If a guy in baseball bats .150, what do you do? Get his ass out of there. You can look at it any way you want to. They thought they had a legitimate point. What's a receiver paid to do? He's paid to catch the ball. I know he doesn't try to drop it, but if he drops it in a critical situation or he fumbles at a critical situation, I think he ought to know about it. You say, "Well, you don't have to tell them on the sideline." Well, somebody does and somebody doesn't. I just tell them, "Hey, we need those kind of plays. It's the difference between winning and losing." It's the same thing I meant in college when the guy said it didn't matter because there would be another chance. There isn't always another chance. That might be the last chance you get to get yourself into the Super Bowl. You have to play every play like it's the last play.

We went to Detroit and got beat 31-17. After they scored in the last couple minutes, I thought they were laughing at us on the sideline. I told Dave Duerson to block their kicker, Eddie Murray. I didn't send him after him; I told him to block him. What did he do? He blocked him. If Eddie wouldn't have ducked, he wouldn't have hurt his shoulder. It wasn't illegal. Everybody said, "You're a criminal for doing it." Why is the kicker protected anyway? In the old days, we used to go after kickers all the time. When I was an assistant in Dallas, we played Green Bay in Milwaukee. Chester Marcol was kicking for them. I told our middle guy on the opening kickoff not to get too deep. If I told him once, I told him a thousand times they were going to onside kick it right in front of him. Here comes Marcol and my guy starts back. Marcol kicks it right where he was and the Packers recover it. I'm ticked off. The Packers go down and kick a field goal. I grabbed my guy. I said, "Kid, you line up 15 yards away from Marcol. When he starts running, you start running. When he hits the ball, you hit him." Well, he hit him. And I can still see Bob Lord, their special teams coach, coming up the sidelines hollering at me. I said, "All's fair in love and war." He really hit Marcol hard. I don't know why that offends everybody. I mean what the hell's so special about a kicker? They just talk different, that's all. If they can make $180,000 or $200,000 to kick, why the hell can't they get dirty? I heard one time when Abe Gibron coached the Bears he sent someone after Marcol and asked whether Marcol thought he was a Polish Prince. Abe and I can relate to each other. Luke Johnsos, who coached with Halas for 30 years, called me up after the Murray thing and said, "I don't know what the hell they're mad about. We used to go after the kicker all the time." Halas had a thing for whoever got the kicker.

On the Saturday before we went to Philadelphia when we were 2-5, I told everyone in the meeting that we didn't have to take everybody. I said: "I don't want anybody going who doesn't think we can win. I don't care if we leave here with 25 people. Anybody who doesn't think we can beat the Eagles, stay home." We went up there and won 7-6. To score only 7 points was atrocious, but if we had lost that game, I don't think I would be around right now. That game had a lot to do with really getting us untracked. They found out that day I didn't really give a darn about their feelings or all the guys who wanted to fight and bitch about this and that. It didn't matter to me anymore, because I knew you couldn't win with those guys anyhow. And most of them aren't here. I'm talking about guys who were selfish. We would get a quarterback sack and they were pointing to their teammates. Noah Jackson did that to Covert. I never saw anything like it. I'd rather have a guy come back and say, "Hey, I blew the play; it was my fault. We'll get them next time." You're not going to beat the guy every time. That's why the guy on the other side is getting paid all that money. But we had guys who would come out of the game and we would ask, "What happened?" They would say, "It wasn't my fault." Now, our kids come out and say, "Mike, we can't block it that way. We have to do something different." They straighten it out with Dick.

Mr. Halas was in and out of the hospital with cancer most of the summer and fall. I went to the hospital all the time. He would be very lucid when he was awake. He asked about the draft and about the players. I told him he would like Covert because he was just like Joe Stydahar. He would smile and say, "That's good." He died on Monday night, Oct. 31, 1983. I can't express what my true feelings were. I didn't know how many friends I had. I knew the one friend I had wasn't here, that's for sure. I knew the one reason I came here wasn't here. I pretty much understood what the hell was going on, which was I was there by myself and the criteria for staying was going to be whether we won or lost. That was what I was going to be judged on. There was nothing to say there even had to be a third year. I don't think it changed my outlook at all because I still felt we had a competitive team. I believed that we were doing the right things, drafting the right way. I wasn't being bothered by anybody in running the football team. But I really never could tell whose support I had and whose I didn't have. I thought I had everybody's support, at least on the outside. How deep that was I don't know.

We went to Los Angeles to play the Rams the next week. McMahon was my quarterback for good. We talked about Coach Halas. I thought one of the things he would have tried to get across was not necessarily that we dedicate a win to him, but just dedicate our effort to him. We got beat in L.A., 21-14, but we didn't get beat because we weren't trying. We played pretty good that day.

The next week I started wearing a tie on the sideline. I just felt like wearing a tie. I had thought about wearing a tie when I first came, but I thought people would compare me to other people. In the old days, every head coach wore a coat and tie. Halas, Lombardi, Allie Sherman, Paul Brown. These days, only Tom Landry did. I thought people would say I was trying to be somebody I wasn't. I've had letters from people saying, "Take off the tie and put on a sweatshirt and be one of the guys." I've had others say, "Leave the tie on; you're not one of the players and you shouldn't dress the same." I started out wearing one with shamrocks on it for good luck. I have all kinds of ties now. I said I hoped it would relax me. That wasn't a real good statement, but it sort of did, not that I didn't get mad when I had a tie on, but I don't think I got as mad with the tie on as I got without it. Maybe it's an authority thing. I know Tom doesn't dress that way on the sidelines to show off the clothes he's wearing. He does it because that's the role he plays, the head coach.

I think everybody's superstitious, but I don't really believe that by doing things a certain way I'm going to be lucky. I do things a certain way because I get into a pattern, like a ritual. We went to Tampa Bay and Jerry Vainisi and I ate alligator meat and we won. So you better believe I'm going to eat alligator meat every time we go to Tampa Bay. We even started serving it on the team plane. I still have trouble remembering whether it's alligator or crocodile.

Nobody respected the players we had more than I did, but when it's time to change, it's time to change. Bob Parsons came to me early in the season saying he was punting terrible and I ought to cut him. I said, "Bob, you're a punter. All you have to do is punt the football and keep your mouth shut. I know you have a temper; I have a temper, too." Then late in the season, I found out he was trying to get a job with the Blitz in the USFL. Why not wait until the season is over? That would have been like me going to the Rams with four games left and saying, "I want to have the job there next year." If my owner found out, he'd fire me. There was a difference between what Parsons did and what I did when I wrote that letter to Halas from Dallas. I wasn't the head coach of the Cowboys. I was a guy who was just trying to improve my employment. I had all the loyalty in the world to the Cowboys. Bob was making a complete lateral move. But players wondered. Doug Plank brought it up on a radio show. A player can perceive it any way he wants to. Plank was a guy who played a lot of years and was a good player. All of a sudden, he has an injury and we're told by doctors he shouldn't play any more and we tell him that and all of a sudden he's mad at me, the coach. I'm the bad guy. That happened with a lot of players. They were mad at me, but the Bears couldn't continue to flounder around in mediocrity. I never had anything against Bob Parsons. I pity punters who have to punt in Chicago year after year. He was kind of a dinosaur to last that long. Did I cut him because of his punting or because of the USFL deal? I could say punting and stand on it, but it wasn't that. I just thought it was time to make a change. Bob had gotten to a point where he really didn't get along with too many guys on the team. He was kind of a pain in the ass. Every time there would be a special teams meeting, there would be a big fight. He would get mad at somebody or somebody would get mad about the special teams. It was crazy. We'd be going to play a game and everybody would be mad at everybody on the special teams. I'd say, "What the hell is going on?" It was time to make a change.

We had to find people who were tired of being also-rans, part of the pack, doormats for Minnesota, Green Bay, or Detroit. A lot of people thought of the Bears as nice guys. They made a nice appearance at the meetings. Just pat those boys on the head. Keep them out of your way. Drop them a bone every once in a while. We went up to Minnesota and my whole talk was how there was no reason in the world that the Bears had not won up there in 11 years. I said, "I don't care who coaches Minnesota or who they have playing for them, it's asinine. In all those 11 years, they weren't a better football team than you guys. But we have a little problem that we can't beat Minnesota in Minnesota. Why don't we try to disprove that?" Everybody for years walked around mesmerized and saying how great the Vikings were in the Central Division. Bullshit. They are no better than anybody else if you play football. We won 19-13.

It bothered me that I didn't get a contract extension past 1984 from Michael McCaskey after the 1983 season. It bothered me a lot. But you're only a part of the system. I felt I needed it to go back to the players and say, "I'm going to be here and this is why we do this and we can proceed forward." Going into 1984, I thought that put a lot of pressure on me. The players were going to play whether I was there or not, but I thought a contract extension would have been good for the assistants and for a lot of other things. I can understand it, though. I wasn't their pick. I talked about it with Michael, but it was a very short conversation as I remember, and very one-sided, also. I still had a year on my contract and I honor my contracts. I was going to do the best I could. We were only 8-8 in 1983, but I knew we had a good football team.

XVII

Platteville—'84

In 1984, we decided to have training camp at the University of Wisconsin-Platteville instead of at Lake Forest. I wanted to get them away from the congestion in Lake Forest. Every time they walked out the door of Halas Hall after practice, there were kids, wives, girlfriends. In Platteville, they were going to do things together. I was hoping we'd have more camaraderie. I think some good things happened.

Jerry Vainisi, our general manager, did an outstanding job of getting everybody signed. We were still making changes. We decided to go with Mark Bortz instead of Noah Jackson at guard. It's easy as a coach to take the easy way out and say we're going to play a guy because he has experience. So what? What about the guy who hasn't played but will give you every bit of fiber and effort and sweat and hustle he has? Let's get his butt out on the field and see how he can play. Bortz turned out to be a darn good football player and we didn't miss Noah. We don't have perfect players by any means, but we have players who are my kind of players, Bear players, Halas's kind of players.

McMahon got hurt in the second game when we beat Denver 27-0. Got his hand broken when he was tackled after throwing a touchdown pass. We went to Green Bay the next week for a big game and he tried to play, but we went with Bob Avellini in the second half. Steve Fuller hurt his shoulder in the preseason. Bob's a nice guy, but he just wouldn't do what we told him to do. We called a play to hit the back going up the middle and it was wide open. He threw the ball outside to somebody and Mark Lee almost intercepted it. I told him on the sideline, "If I wasn't in the predicament I'm in, I'd fire your ass."

I also said when he started in Seattle the next week if he would just go in and do what we say we could win with him. I backed him all the way. But he had to audible when we were ahead 7-0 and they intercepted and ran it back for a touchdown. That's when I asked him whether he liked me. I said, "Don't you like your teammates? Do you think we're stupid that we don't give you good plays? I mean, why would you do that?" I didn't understand and neither did Ed Hughes and neither did any of our coaches and neither did the Seattle coaching staff why the hell he audibled. The Seahawks were tickled to death to see it, but they didn't understand it. Things happen for a reason. It got Bob back to New York. We cut him a week later and the Jets picked him up.

McMahon tried to come back against Dallas and we lost 23-14. We ran for a lot of yards in the first half and then they gave us the pass and Jim's hand wasn't good enough to throw the ball. We put in Rusty Lisch and he couldn't pass either. All they did was make one change in how they were playing our off-tackle run. We were killing them with it. What we should have done is just made a simple adjustment and started running inside or running all the way outside. We missed two field goals in the first half and we couldn't even kill the clock. McMahon tried to throw a ball out of bounds and Willie Gault caught it. We couldn't execute the simplest passes in the second half. Then afterwards, I gave my short press conference. Yes. No. Next question. One guy's questions were asinine. I don't even remember what he was asking. Did I get outcoached? Sure, I got outcoached. That game bothered me more than any of them. Maybe it was that I had played in Dallas and coached in Dallas and this was our first game against them. I might have been a little selfish from that point of view. But I felt we really matched up well with them.

I didn't get on players on the sidelines much in 1984. The only guys who really upset me were the quarterbacks. We had to start five different quarterbacks—McMahon, Avellini, Lisch, Fuller, and Greg Landry. I only got mad at Steve once and that was against the Rams when he didn't throw to Matt Suhey when he was open. Greg played super for us. I got mad at Avellini some and I got mad at Lisch in the San Diego game for carrying the ball like a loaf of bread and getting it knocked out of his hands.

I think the players understand now that when I say something bad, it only lasts for two seconds and it's forgotten. When I praise them, it lasts a lot longer. I got some heat in the St. Louis game for playing some other people for Suhey and Jay Saldi, our tight end. Anybody could see there were key plays that were missed and should have been made. How do you bench a guy? You just do it. Then you wait for someone to knock on the door and the player comes in and tells you how great he is and how you're making a mistake taking him out.

I think we have good communication. I started a board

with the captains and some veterans that meets every week to find out what they think about practices and the way everything is going. I got the idea from Tom. He used to meet with the captains and use them as a sounding board. I tell them my feelings about the upcoming game and what I think they have to impart to their teammates if we don't get it across as coaches. They tell me what they don't like. They need a microwave in their lounge. They need phones in the locker room. "How come we have to autograph all the balls?" "Why can't we get paid for autographing the balls?" "Why can't we do appearances during the season?" Most of the time, there's very little bitching. Most of the time I just try to get across to them the strong points of our opponents and how we have to attack them. I want to try to get them to impart it in their own way to their teammates. Then I talk to everybody on Saturday night and before the game on Sunday in the locker room and tell them the same thing. What I'm trying to do is really make them understand and believe that what I'm saying is important so they can carry the message.

I don't enjoy fining players. First of all, the collective bargaining rules don't allow you to fine them enough to hurt. And that's money away from them and their family. If I thought a guy did something really wrong, I'd fine him. All the money goes to charity.

I got fined after the St. Louis game for commenting on the officials. The play that made me furious was when Otis Wilson was called for roughing their quarterback, Neil Lomax. Lomax pushed him first. I said something right after the game and then on Monday the press started it back up again. I felt they egged me on. They pulled it out of me. But they didn't pull very hard since I was going to say it anyway. Then I got a letter from the commissioner and the fine. I'm sure it won't be the last time I'll be fined. I just think the officials have an obligation to the coaches to explain why things are called a certain way. But they won't talk to you. We prepare all year for these games. It's an ongoing process through April, May, June, July. Then because of one silly call in October, it keeps you from going to the Super Bowl. Just give me an explanation. They're human and we're human. I'm interviewed five minutes after the game and nobody asks the officials anything. They're the sons of guns who make the calls.

We beat the Raiders 17-6. I've never been around a game that was that hard-hitting. It was a great confidence-builder. When you're climbing the ladder, you have to have games like that. The San Francisco game in 1983 was like that. You have to beat those upper echelon teams. When we beat the Raiders after they were Super Bowl champs, Al Davis said the game was our Super Bowl. That's not wrong. When you're king of the hill, people try to knock you off. That's what it's all about. That's why you have to respect teams like Miami, the Raiders, Dallas, and Pittsburgh who have climbed up there and stayed up there over the years and turned away the slings and arrows. When you can continue to win after everybody is after you, that's a great sign. You've learned something about mental toughness and how to perform under pressure.

We ended up losing McMahon and Leslie Frazier, our cornerback, for the season against the Raiders. I felt we could continue to win if we played our kind of football, if we played a low-risk offense and our defense.

Two weeks later, after we beat Detroit to go to an 8-4 record, I went on the radio and said there was a good chance I wouldn't be back as coach in 1985. I was answering a question and I tried to answer it honestly, except I was so tired I guess it didn't come out right. But at that point, I didn't know. Nobody ever told me. Nobody ever walked up and said, "Hey, you're doing a heck of a job." Or, "You're doing O.K." The only thing I had to base anything on was the record. We knew the record was good enough, but you don't know how other people perceive that. They might perceive it as, "Well, the record should be good; we've got good personnel." I had to wonder a little bit, but I didn't say what I said to precipitate anything. I said it out of weariness with no idea it could cause that much furor. But everybody is looking for a scoop, so they made a big deal out of nothing. Maybe I had some self-pity involved in my answer, I don't know. I was tired and the guy was almost crying on the phone when he asked the question, saying, "We'll never be fans again" and this and that. All I meant was, "You have to be realistic. The guy who hired me is no longer here. If they want to make a change, they're certainly entitled to make that change." It could happen at any time. When you're in this business, you can't fool yourself. Whether I think I'm a good coach or a bad coach, I'm going to be judged on one thing: record. But winning and not knowing anything started bothering me a little bit.

Before our first playoff game against the Redskins, we had a two-week layoff and that's when the contract was first talked about. It wasn't like I had the upper hand on anybody. I couldn't say, "Hey, I've got a great job in business." Or, "I've got a great possibility in coaching somewhere else." I wasn't going to do that. I wanted to stay here. Maybe that's a weakness, but maybe that's a strength. It's certainly a weakness when it comes time for negotiating. But it's a strength when it comes to dedicating yourself. It is still one of the smallest contracts in the league, but it doesn't matter. I'm not underpaid. The new contract was announced the week before the NFC championship game in San Francisco. I wish McCaskey wouldn't have done it at that particular time. I didn't think it would help the players' morale and it wasn't going to help my morale.

The win in Washington was exciting. It was a great game, good for football. We went down there and beat a good football team in their back yard. That's not easy to do. I thought it gave us national recognition as a tough football team. It's the way Halas would have wanted it. I felt I had paid the first installment for the confidence he showed in bringing me back. I said I thought somewhere he was smiling pretty good.

XVIII

Highs and Lows—'85

Not to be able to score a point in a championship game was a great embarrassment. The 49ers beat us 23-0
and went on to win Super Bowl XIX. I just didn't think they
were that much of a better football team. I don't care who we
had on the field. We had Steve Fuller at quarterback, but I
take the blame for the way we attacked them. The loss hurt
Walter a lot. It hurt Gary Fencik. It hurt a lot of those guys a
lot. We vowed to go back. The 49ers said in the papers we
ought to bring an offense the next time. I said we would have a
passing game. That loss was a tremendous catalyst for our
1985 season.

We played them in the sixth game. The first thing I said on
the Monday after we beat Tampa Bay to go 5-0 was: "Get

ready for a war. I don't want anybody smiling around here. We're going to get ready to go to war." We had one hell of a week of practice. When we got out there, we were ready to fly. The 49ers didn't respect us. How could they respect us? They had just beaten us 23-0 six months earlier. We played without starting receivers Dennis McKinnon and Emery Moorehead, but we played pretty good. That last quarter of football made us a good offense, when we took the football and ran it when we had to run it. We beat them 26-10.

I celebrated too much. I was arrested and later convicted of drunk driving. It was the most embarrassing thing that could ever happen to me. I was stopped on I-294 shortly after leaving O'Hare airport. I was driving home. The officer handcuffed me and I didn't think it was necessary. But when it's all said and done, whether it could have been avoided by the officer or by me is beside the point. It happened. It was embarrassing because it surprised me. I didn't consider myself to be intoxicated. Now, after learning more about it, I'm sure I was. But you always feel you're handling yourself pretty well.

I had breakfast before the game. We played the game. We got on the plane and I never had a bit of food. We were at 40,000 feet. I was drinking white wine. If a lot is two bottles, then I had more than a lot. It's a four-hour flight. You sit down and you drink a glass of wine. You're dehydrated. You're excited. You're flushed from the game. You've been out in the sun all day. I drank it like water for the first five or six drinks. Then I thought I was O.K. I really did. I still argue that I wasn't that bad, but I guess technically or legally I knew I drank too much. It was a matter of trying to get the car to where I was going, which was home to bed. I didn't make it.

I always used to say and hear other people say, "I don't drink hard stuff, so that doesn't make me a drinker." That's wrong. Once you understand that it does make you drunk, I don't care if you drink beer, wine, or whatever, you're still drinking. You get the same thing out of it—alcohol. I don't drink hard stuff. I drink wine and I like champagne a lot. How many times a week do I drink? Once, basically. Sometimes none, sometimes twice. When do I drink? Usually when I'm with people I like and usually to celebrate something. I never drink at home alone and rarely drink at home, period. I don't have a drinking problem and I know that's true after taking classes in the Alcohol Safety Education Program. But it's something you've got to be aware of, especially a person who is in my position. I have an obligation to the public and to young people. I have talked to kids in schools about drinking. I'm of the age to drink. It still amazes me that we say alcohol is acceptable and legal, but drugs aren't, when there's no difference in how they affect the body and the mind. It's something you think about when you learn about it. It's something you try to tell kids. I'm 46 years old. I'm an adult. I have a right to drink. That's my business if I want to do it. But I don't have a right to drink and drive. That right nobody has. If I'm going to be jeopardizing my life and the lives of others and of other people's property, then I don't have the right to drive. I understand that very well now. I think that everything works for the best and I think that what happened was probably for the best. It educated me about a couple things I really didn't know about. And I feel good about it now. I had resentment at first. It bothered me. The officer bothered me. I resented him. I don't any more. He did his job and that's it.

If this is the worst thing that ever happens to me and the worst thing I ever do, I might get a humanitarian of the year award. There are some people who want to make it a bigger deal than it is. There are some so-called Christians—and I'm a Christian—who want to say, "Ho ho, we got this hypocrite. We caught him." That's fine with me. I don't answer. My judgement is not going to be made by any of those people. It's the guy upstairs. And I'm sure the first thing he's going to say to me is, "Aha! I remember you that night of October 14, you were drunk. You can't come in for that." That isn't going to be the case at all, because it's not going to mean anything.

I got some letters. Some of the stupid ones from goofballs kind of hurt me. I got more letters supporting me, but even some of those said they were going to do this and that to the state trooper, which is silly, too. He was only doing his job. When we went to Green Bay a couple weeks later, they had signs up: "This Bud's for you, presented by the Illinois State Trooper's Association." They have a lot of classy fans in Green Bay.

Two coaches called me—Tom Landry and Dan Reeves. It meant a lot because it was such an embarrassment and you blow everything out of perspective because you think you're the only one who has ever done it.

I quit drinking after the arrest. I didn't have anything until our victory over the Giants in the first game of the playoffs.

There were a lot of highlights during the season and one of our biggest wins was the opener against Tampa Bay and the way we won it 38-28. People thought we would come out and shut them down, score 7 or 10 points and win. If we got behind, the Bears weren't a team that came from behind very well. But they scored, we scored, they scored. We were behind 21-7 and 28-17 at the half. Then Leslie Frazier made that big interception and touchdown to start the second half. Their coach, Leeman Bennett, said he had watched all our exhibition films and thought they had a much better team than the Bears had. "We really thought we'd beat you without any problem," he said. It really hurt their season. We finished 15-1 and they finished 2-14 and not many teams attacked our defense better than Tampa Bay did two times. Without question, if you don't win the first game, you're starting from behind the 8-ball. Go back to 1983. If we had beaten Atlanta, we would have been 9-7 instead of 8-8. Detroit won the division that year at 9-7. The opener is what it's all about.

The players wanted to be known as a special team in 1985 and they played hard every week to prove it. They play hard because I think they know they have to play hard to stay on the field. There's nobody I wouldn't replace. We had already proven that. And we were winning minus holdouts that people said we couldn't win without—that we could not play without. It all goes back to personal pride. They hadn't forgotten the San Francisco game and they didn't put Tampa Bay on any different level. The Bucs were good because they were in the NFL.

I was probably as proud after the Jets' game as any all year. We had already clinched the home field advantage. It was the second-to-last game of the year. We could have jumped into a shell and protected ourselves, but we went out there to win a football game and play hard. We played with a lot of pride and a lot of heart in conditions that weren't that good.

We emphasized playing with a chip on the shoulder. Make the other guy's all-opponent team. Put the chip up there and make the other guy knock it off. I heard that expression growing up. You can say it a thousand ways but it all means the same thing: get ready to play. That's the way football should be played. People ask what the game will be like in the year 2,000. If it's any different, it won't be football. I mean if they're going to throw the ball 60 times a game, that's stupid. Football is football. It was a pretty good game 60 years ago and it's a pretty good game today.

I believe it's important that you be the underdog, to make your team realize they're not the fair-haired boys and they're not liked. We went into Dallas and that was my whole approach. They didn't respect us. They were going to kick our ass.

Going in, there was no question in my mind we were going

to win the game. But of course the year before there was no question in my mind we were going to win and we didn't. I just felt we could do more against their defense than they could do against our defense. The most important thing about the game was we knew we had to play good on defense to help the offense. It was just an outstanding effort by everyone. We got after them a little bit. Steve Fuller ran the team very well at quarterback and got the support he needed. When it was over, I said to Coach Landry I was sorry for the way it ended. We had reserves in the game and scored two times. He said he understood. Usually, when you get into a blowout, there's nothing you can do. Guys are trying to prove things. We had a lot of guys from Texas playing and their families were there. I'm not sure the Cowboys didn't give up a little bit, too. They were beat up and their offensive line had a lot of injuries.

It wasn't a special feeling to beat them that bad. It was a good feeling because we hadn't beaten them since 1971, when I played for the Cowboys. It wasn't because I wanted to go back and prove anything. That never bothered me. I don't have to prove anything to people in Dallas. I have a lot of friends there who like me and I have a lot of people there who think I'm an asshole. So what? It's even. It's probably the same in Chicago, Philadelphia, and Pittsburgh. The game made us 10-0. It was the one game that convinced me. Afterwards, I said: "We're a good football team. We're not just an average football team." But did you see what the Cowboys said afterwards? They said they didn't play well. We used that all year. "You beat Dallas 44-0 and they never said you were a good team. They just said it was your night, that they didn't play well."

The next day, Mike Richardson made his remark about people on the defense offering to buy lunches for anybody who knocked out a quarterback. Otis Wilson had knocked Danny White out of the game twice. There is no such thing as a bounty. It was just conversation. The object of the defense is to get pressure on the quarterback. I told Mike and everybody else that stuff like that sounds cute in the locker room, but if you expose it to everybody else it makes us look like we're dirty. And we're not dirty. We're just a good football team and we play hard. Mike came up to see me right away and said he didn't mean it like that. I told him not to worry about it. But we got letters about it from Rozelle. I didn't think it was that important. I know we go out to hit them hard, but that's football. We got crap from Green Bay about blocking Lynn Dickey after an interception. The first thing defenses are taught is to block the quarterback after an interception. He's the last line of support. We ran a touchdown back against Minnesota and old Perry knocked the beans out of Tommy Kramer. My goodness gracious, you've got to do those things. That's only part of football.

When Wilber Marshall was fined $2,000 for hitting Joe Ferguson in Detroit, I thought it was a legitimate tackle. Against the Colts, Coach Rod Dowhower thought Marshall tried to wipe a guy's leg out. We got a letter from Rozelle on that. I told Marshall, "Don't ever do it again." Marshall told me the guy did something to him three plays before that. I said, "Don't ever do it again. We don't coach it. We don't teach it. We don't condone it. I'll fire you in a minute for it." I told him that in front of the whole football team.

We wanted to beat every team in our division twice. We were thinking about that, but I don't think we ever really got to thinking about 8-0, 9-0, 10-0, 11-0, 12-0. I don't think it meant anything. The first thing is they went out there for the enjoyment of playing. Then the second thing is they enjoyed whipping up on people. Then they liked to see the scoreboard in their favor. If you play and get after them, the third thing usually works out. In the end, they even enjoyed practice. Not

every one of them, but I think overall we really enjoyed practicing. That was good because that's where you really accomplish things.

I thought the only way we could lose was if we turned the
ball over on offense or didn't play our positions on defense.
That's what happened to us in Miami. They had a little better
game plan than we had. Give them credit. We were outcoached. I heard a guy say afterwards how badly we were outcoached. I agreed. When we came out, Steve Fuller was a little
nervous. We missed our first couple passes. We were going to
run the ball. They started jumping the defenses on us and we
missed blocks. That's why we started throwing it. What happens when you start getting behind is you keep thinking you
have to catch up and you get away from the running game. It
was during that game that the TV cameras caught me and
Mike Singletary yelling. I was hollering, "Hey, we can win this
game." He was hollering, "I know we're going to win it." It
had nothing to do with screaming at him. We didn't give up.

We started getting into commercials and the "Super Bowl
Shuffle" after we wrapped up the division and the home field
advantage. I wasn't worried about them being a distraction until the last game in Detroit and then I really got mad about the
way we played up there. We were on our way toward something
special and we didn't play very smart up there. Whether they
liked it or not, I was going to tell them to back off. I didn't
want anything said or done until after the playoffs, so I
jumped on them. It was never a problem. I thought they handled it super. If we hadn't wrapped up everything, I would have
said no. They told me about the "Super Bowl Shuffle" and I
said fine, if it's for charity. Even if it wasn't for charity, I wasn't
going to say no. They did it on their time off. They asked me to
be in it and I said, "Nope."

The playoffs were a big challenge. The Giants and Rams

were two good football teams. We just made some plays they didn't make. There wasn't any great disparity in ability. The home field advantage had a tremendous bearing on what happened in those games. The anticipation of getting ready every week was exciting. I called our team the Grabowskis before the Rams' game. It just came out. I could have said Dombrowski, but I said Grabowski. I think people understood it. I think they thought that was a pretty good analogy for our football team.

XIX

The "Red" Bay Packers

I know there's no love lost between the Green Bay Packers and the Chicago Bears and that's the way it should be. Respect them. Play them hard. But I don't want to be buddy-buddy with the Packers and they don't want to be buddy-buddy with us. That's the way it was through the 60s, but there was a great respect between George Halas and Vince Lombardi. Tremendous respect. I just know that I respect the rivalry between the two teams. That's all I can say about it. I don't like a lot of things that happened in our rivalry with them in 1985, but that's part of the game.

In our game in Green Bay November 3 after we beat them October 21 in Chicago, they came out to hurt some people. They came out to beat us the way they thought they could beat us and it didn't work. If that's what they think they can do to beat the Bears—intimidate us—they have another thought coming. They better get some better football players before they try to do that.

When Ken Stills hit Matt Suhey long after the play was over, Lombardi would have fired that guy right there. He never taught it, never condoned it, and never would have put up with that bullshit. Forrest Gregg called it "aggressive football." Suhey challenged Forrest in a restaurant in New Orleans during Super Bowl week. He asked him, "Do you coach that kind of football?" Forrest didn't know what to say.

Commissioner Rozelle fined Ken Stills $500 for that hit and fined Wilber Marshall $2,000 for his hit against Joe Ferguson. I'll defend Marshall's hit the rest of my life. I think it was a great example of how to play the game and a poor example of how to legislate the game.

I don't have any feud with Forrest. I played with him for a year in Dallas and I played in the Pro Bowl with him. I just don't like some of the things that have happened. In our last exhibition game with them in 1984 in Milwaukee, there were 30-some seconds left in the half and they called a time out. We had the ball and we were going to run it out. I just thought it was kind of silly to call a time out in an exhibition game. I got a little mad about it. I said, "That was an asshole thing to do to call a time out in an exhibition game." I guess one of Forrest's assistants told him about it. In the locker room, Forrest told his team, "You take care of the Bears; I'll take care of Ditka."

I like Forrest. I'm a lot like Forrest in a lot of ways. He speaks his mind; I speak my mind. I think he's a hell of a coach, but that doesn't mean I don't think it's stupid to call a time out with 30 seconds left in the half of an exhibition game. We gained 9 yards after the time out and Calvin Thomas hurt his leg on the play. In a league game, you can call 300 time outs anytime you want to.

In the third week of the 1984 season, we talked before the game and I told Forrest what a great day for football I thought it was. Clear sky, natural grass, nice stadium, close to the fans, great fall day, Bears and Packers. To me, that is the epitome of the way NFL games should be played.

Lombardi was an influence on me. I played for him in two Pro Bowls and got to know him. Through his players, he paid me a great compliment as a young player. He said, "If we're going to beat the Bears, we have to stop this guy." That meant a lot to me. To me, that's what life is all about, when you're appreciated by your peers, when the people you're around and play against recognize your talent. Being recognized by sportswriters, excuse me, doesn't mean shit. Let's face it. It doesn't mean crapola.

When I was a rookie, I had a good game against Green Bay and they beat us 31-28. I think I had three touchdowns. It took time to get confidence in how well you could play against the Packers back then. We used to call them the Red Bay Packers because every time we said Green Bay, the coaches choked. I'm not sure if it was the coaches or the players who choked. Halas had some great names for the Packers, but he had great respect for Lombardi. They had set the precedent. You had to beat them to be the champions. When we beat them twice in 1963, including the opener in Green Bay, those were two of the greatest memories I had as a player. When we beat them 26-7 in Wrigley Field, I don't remember the incidents in that game, but I remember the feeling. To beat a team like that, you really had to be playing good football. Bart Starr got hurt in that game. Our defense went after them and our offense controlled the ball. Nobody had really done that to the Packers.

I could tell that the Pro Bowl wasn't Lombardi's cup

of tea. It was the lack of discipline in the situation. You could tell it annoyed him tremendously. But he went along with the flow of things. He liked to go to the racetrack as well as anybody else. Guys would practice early and head for Santa Anita. Some would head for the bar and that's where they basically stayed until they went to bed. A lot of guys played golf. That was not his cup of tea. He could have controlled anything he wanted, but it was the spirit of the game to run it loosely. One year, we won and played very well. The next year, we got annihilated by the East. I think John Brodie threw six interceptions. It was just crazy. Lombardi had great restraint on the sideline. I don't think I ever saw anybody use self-restraint to a greater degree than he did that day. Even though the game meant nothing, it meant something to him. There was a personal pride involved. He was coaching this team. That's when I said to myself, "This guy is something special." I think anybody who says losing is O.K. is going to be a loser. By saying losing isn't O.K. doesn't mean you're going to win every one either. I think if you say it's O.K. if you lose, then you're going to be the guy that when the chips are on the table, you're going to get beat. That's all there is to it. That's the way he was. Losing at anything wasn't something he would enjoy and I guess that's why I respected him so much. And I also respected him because of the way he controlled himself.

Everybody talks about the quote he had about "winning isn't everything; it's the only thing." I think he was talking about the effort to win. Not only that, I think he was saying that sometimes it's not winning that's everything, but how do you deal with defeat? What do you do when things don't go your way? When things are going your way, it's easy to live with your wife, your family, your coaches, the players, the sportswriters.

He also said something that stuck with me after he left

Green Bay and went to Washington in 1969. There was a lot of unrest in society and on campuses at that time. They were burning flags and draft cards and a lot of dopeheads were coming into football. He said: "It's become increasingly difficult to be tolerant of a society that only has sympathy for misfits, the maladjusted, criminals, and losers. It's about time in our society that we stood up and cheered for the doers, the achievers, and people who recognize the problems and do something about them." He said that we should pity and help the losers and criminals, but let's give credit where credit is due, to the people who are out there getting it done, to the people who don't come with the problems, but who come with the solutions. To me, that's a sound philosophy about everything.

There are great stories about the Bear-Packer rivalry. Before I came, I was told the Bears were stealing the Packers' signals in the 1980 game when the Bears won 61-7. I don't believe in spending time trying to steal signals, but if anybody is smart enough to steal signals in football, baseball, basketball, hockey, or anything else, let them do it. With all the film exchange nowadays, it doesn't pay to spend time stealing signals or spying, but I believe it probably happens in our league today. I know it happened when I played. Halas had two sets of film, one in focus and one slightly out of focus. You can imagine which one the opposition got. I'm sure Halas used to spy on people and he was always afraid someone was spying on him. Doug Atkins used to get the Old Man at Wrigley Field. He would bring a .22 to the park and shoot pigeons. He'd be walking around and all of a sudden he'd yell, "Hey, there's somebody up there watching us!" Then he would shoot the pigeons. We had security people all over Wrigley Field when we practiced. Cops and Andy Frain ushers would be running around, trying to see who was spying.

One time, the Rams had to play at Green Bay, Chicago,

and Detroit. They would stay in Milwaukee between the
games. When Joe Marconi played for the Rams, he said their
coach, Hamp Pool, used to be afraid of spies. They would get
on the bus to go to practice, start driving, and all of a sudden
Pool would say, "Stop the bus." They would get off the bus
and there would be a park or lot and they would start practicing. They would practice for half an hour and jump back on
the bus, drive, go to another lot, jump out, and start practicing
again. Damndest thing he ever saw.

When we beat the Packers in Chicago on the Monday
night that Perry scored, we got criticized by the announcers
and by their coaches for rubbing it in. People can think what
they want to think. I've always made the statement that if a
team beats me 45-0, that's their business. Fine, run it up. Do
anything you want. That's football. What are you supposed to
do? All of a sudden, are you supposed to start saying, "We
shouldn't do this. We have to play these guys again"? I said after our first game if they didn't like it they could do something
about it in two weeks. That's just the way I feel. And they came
out after us the second time, no question about it. It was our
closest win of the year, 16-10. Perry scored on a pass from Jim
McMahon and it couldn't have come against a greater group of
guys in a better situation. I didn't plan it for them, but that's
where I wanted it. The way that game went that day, it was
kind of fitting. There was a little bit of "Here, take this," involved.

Walter Payton ran as well that game as anyone I had ever
seen, because he had to run through some people. The Packers
were playing the "46" defense and we weren't doing a whole
lot of other things. We had to rely on Walter's running ability.

Before the game, we found a bag of manure in our locker
room sent by some radio station. Nothing in Green Bay sur-
prises me. I put it right out in the middle of the locker room
where everybody could see it.

Right after the game, I jumped all over Otis Wilson because he got a 15-yard penalty after we had stopped them on a third down. We had just gone ahead of them halfway through the fourth quarter. It gave them a first down.

I didn't get mad about a whole lot of things, but I got mad about that because it was a reflection on the whole team and coaching staff. Maybe some coaches like it. I don't. That's why I yelled at Richard Dent for fighting in the Minnesota game when the microphone picked me up swearing at him. All I was saying was, "Get him the heck off the field." I just think it's wrong. I don't like to be known as a team that gets a lot of penalties. They make you look stupid and make you look like bad coaches. I like to be known as a team that knocks the crap out of people.

Those two wins over Green Bay were two of our toughest games of the year. They always are. I'm looking forward to it next year because we'll play them a little bit differently. We may just go up there with baseball bats.

PROFILES

XX

McMahon

Jim McMahon hurt his neck somehow before the second game of the season against the Patriots. We had a game the following Thursday night against the Vikings in Minnesota. He kept saying he was going to be able to play, but he wasn't going to be able to practice. On Tuesday, he sat at practice with Joe Namath, who was in town to do a story on him for ABC. It bothered me, but at that point I didn't think he was going to play in the game anyway. I thought it was a stupid thing to do to sit in the bleachers while the rest of the team was practicing. As a matter of fact, it will be a cold day in hell before Namath gets back on that practice field. Or anybody gets out there. If they want to do something, it will be after practice, not during. That was my fault for letting it happen and I take the blame.

On Thursday, we were in Minnesota and now he had an infection on his leg and he couldn't even get out of bed. Then I knew he wasn't going to play. Steve Fuller was ready, so we decided to go with Steve. No problem. We had a team meeting on Thursday and McMahon wasn't there, so I sent the trainer up to get him. "Tell him to come down. I don't care what he's doing," I said. "He comes to all the meetings." I think it pissed him off. He couldn't really get around on that leg, but I made him come down, limping. Then, I don't know what they did to him, but he came out on the field before the game and he was running around throwing the ball.

The game was amazing, lucky, ridiculous, all of those things. Jim was asking when I was going to put him in. Steve was playing pretty good, but we were behind 17-9 halfway through the third quarter. So I put Jim in and the first play was unbelievable. He got blitzed. Willie Gault looked in, didn't see him, and ran deep. McMahon couldn't throw it when he looked in because he was backing away from a guy, so he waited and threw it deep and Willie was there. Touchdown. We don't have adjustments like that. We look in and throw the ball. But Willie broke clear and he threw deep and it's a touchdown. Little bit lucky. Then his second play, he rolled out and hit Dennis McKinnon for a touchdown. Then on his seventh play, he hit McKinnon again for a touchdown. In the span of 6:40, he completed five of seven passes for three touchdowns and we won 33-24. The next day he was back in the hospital because of his leg infection. The game didn't change my belief on practice. Anyone who thinks he can play without practicing is a fool.

The injury-prone question on Jim is ridiculous. First of all, he plays the game at quarterback like nobody has ever played the game at quarterback before. Nobody. Maybe some started out doing it for two weeks, then they got out of it after they got nailed. He just doesn't care. He's going to do what he has to do to get the job done. If it requires doing things that are a little more dangerous, he'll do them. Here's a guy who was almost out of football with a kidney injury in 1984, then he gets in the Super Bowl and a guy hits him and he does a flip in the air. I don't think he ever thinks about it. He just does it. He did think about sliding a couple of times after we told him to, but now I know he'll never slide again after he got hit in the ass in the playoff game against the Rams.

You've got to get dirty. His teammates love him for that reason. Did you see that picture of him on the sideline after he came out of the Super Bowl? He had his knee pads rolled down, his shirt hanging out, his headband around his neck, his ass pad sticking out, his rib pad unfastened. He looked like a lineman; he didn't look like a quarterback.

He's a winner. The only thing he wants to do is show people he can get it done and win games. He thinks he's our best passer, our best runner, our best blocker, our best tackler. He doesn't do anything halfway.

We scored a lot of touchdowns on his audibles, which we put in the first day of training camp. People were blitzing us to stop the run. He loves it. He really has a great mind. When he sees something on film or Ed Hughes tells him, he recognizes it right away in a game. In the Washington game, they had a safety blitz and the safety was sneaking up to the line. There was no key that he was blitzing, but Jim audibled anyway and hit Emery Moorehead for a touchdown. Emery asked him, "How did you know to audible that?" Jim said, "I could see it in his eyes." He loves to audible. In the Super Bowl, he audibled that pass to Kenny Margerum at the half-yard line. Kenny didn't know what the audible was, so Kenny was standing at the line of scrimmage motioning down and in. Jim yelled "No, down and out." He threw it and it should have been a touchdown.

Jim is different. Everybody was in agreement that we needed to draft a quarterback in my first year. When he walked into my office on draft day with a beer in his hand, I knew he wasn't out to impress anybody here with good manners or good behavior. If Jim would have had any kind of exhibition season, I would have started him. But Bob Avellini played better than any of the others in the preseason. After the strike, we went with McMahon. In 1983, I made a mistake and switched between McMahon and Vince Evans. I kind of buckled to the pressures from the media and the pressures of things not going right. When we lost to the Vikings in Chicago and dropped to 2-4, I yanked Jim for blowing a simple read. He threw an interception dead in the guy's hands when he was rolling up. We practiced that. Jim didn't have his best day, but as it was, it was a big mistake to yank him. I kind of put myself behind the 8-ball to play the other guy.

I started Vince for the next three games, two against Detroit. We lost the two Detroit games, but we beat Philadelphia 7-6 in a game that was a turning point. But the only time we'd ever beaten Detroit was with McMahon at quarterback in the game after the 1982 strike. In 1983, we played them twice and got our butt kicked both times and didn't even have him on the field until the end of the second game. That's not too smart. I just thought at that point Jim wasn't concentrating on what the heck he was supposed to do. But it was a mistake, no question. We couldn't win with the other guy, period. We went with Jim for good starting with the Rams' game, Nov. 6, 1983, the first game after Halas died. Through the Super Bowl, we won 26 of 30 games he started.

Jim is one of the finest competitors I've ever met. He's an individual, outspoken. He doesn't always agree with you and he'll tell you when he doesn't. There's a lot of things in him that are just like I was when I was young and probably like Halas when he was young. Even when he cut his own hair at the 1985 training camp, I remembered when I tried that once at training camp. Mine was accidental, though. I had a crewcut anyway and I tried to trim it. I screwed up, so I put the razor on quarter-inch high and did my whole head. Looked like a bowling ball with fuzz on it. But burr haircuts in those days were acceptable. Mohawks today like Jim had are a little different.

He'll learn as he goes through life what's important and what isn't. You know where you stand with Jim. He doesn't really cuddle up to you. That doesn't bother me. I also know he's going to give you everything he's got. Sometimes, that's a shortcoming, because he tries to make every play a good play. But he'll learn. It was encouraging to watch his improvement during the last season. In the fifth game when we played in the heat in Tampa, he didn't play his best in the first half and we were behind 12-3. I asked him at halftime, "What'd you do last night?" He said, "Nothing." He didn't even know who I was he was so red in the face. I talked with Jim as the season grew to see how involved he was in the games. He got more and more involved and knew what was going on.

After his neck and leg injuries the week of the Minnesota game, I said I thought he could go for a long time and not get hurt again, because injuries go in cycles. I said that one day we'll wake up in a green valley and a stream will be flowing through and all bodies will be healthy and we'll go on to a higher and better life. But it wasn't long afterwards that his shoulder started bothering him. We came pretty darn close to surgery. We thought he was going to have to get the operation until Dr. Michael Schaffer recommended cortisone. He said the joint would be sore as heck and he wouldn't be able to do anything for a week or two. But he thought surgery would find nothing, because he thought it was just an irritated rotator cuff. We were kind of in a quandary. We didn't know what the hell to do. He wasn't getting any better and he was getting depressed about it. We were depressed about it and I guess it was just a matter of thinking, "Well, why don't we go in and take a look?" It might have knocked him out for the season. We were probably a day away from doing it. When you look at things like that, you've really got to believe someone was looking down on us.

When we went to Dallas and played Steve, Jim was on the sidelines in an outfit he called street clothes. They were dead-end street clothes. John Madden said it best: "Those jeans have had a lot of wear." If he would have taken them off, they would have walked around the stadium themselves. I called him into my office the next week and said, "Not on the side-line. From now on, if you're going to stand on the sideline, dress properly. First of all, I want you on the field. But if you have to be on the sideline, dress appropriately." It didn't bother him because he doesn't care. Next time, he'll probably come out in a priest's outfit, like he wore on the plane to Minnesota. He said he didn't do anything to shock anybody. He did things that shocked himself sometimes. He said he really doesn't pre-plan things; he just does them. He's truly a free soul.

When Joe Theismann ripped him after the season about being a poor example, Jim said young people have the right to make up their own minds about the way they want to dress and the way they want to live their lifestyle. It was interesting. I think it's bad for any athlete to come out and be hard on any-body else, because we've all got skeletons. Jim loves his wife, loves his family. He's a great guy about those things. He takes those kids everywhere. He idolizes them. He's a little flaky in some other areas, but that's his business. His family values are about as good as you can get. He doesn't like other quarter-backs that well, but he doesn't put them down. He never says anything bad about his teammates. He's too busy saying derogatory things about me.

That Minnesota game gave us confidence. Afterwards, I figured we were a good enough football team that we weren't going to get beat unless we beat ourselves.

When we woke up before the game on Thursday, we read in the Minneapolis paper that Bud Grant was making a big deal about how his team stood at attention for the national anthem and other teams stood around and scratched themselves. It was my whole pregame speech. I said, "Fellas, I always thought it wasn't so much how you stood, it was what you felt when they played the music. I mean, do you feel good about it? Do you feel patriotic?" They all said yes. "Well I do, too. Let's all take our headgears and put them under our left arms and put our right hands over our hearts. You don't ever want to be upstaged in anything in life."

XXI

The Refrigerator

I challenged William Perry the night before the Super Bowl. He was going to play against John Hannah, the Patriots' guard who was called the best offensive lineman who ever played by *Sports Illustrated* a few years ago. I challenged William right to his face in front of the whole team. I said, "I don't know what your feelings about life are, but if I was you tomorrow, on the first play I'd knock his headgear off. I'd make it a point to knock it off three more times before the game was over." I said to him, "I'd let him know who was boss, who the big fat kid on the block was." I said to him, "You can do what you want to do, Bill, but I'd go out to whip his ass."

You saw the results. Ask John Hannah. If he's All-World,

then what the hell is Perry? He's All-Satellite. Perry came a long way. Dale Haupt, our defensive line coach, really helped him and coached him well. The kid knew nothing about pass rushing. He just pushed people to the quarterback. Now he knows different techniques—arm drags, the "swim"—and he's getting better and better.

When Buddy Ryan called him a wasted draft choice two days after he reported to camp, I sloughed it off by laughing and saying it kind of made me look like an idiot because I was the guy who picked him. I showed great restraint because I wanted to kill Buddy. It really hurt, and it hurt Bill Tobin more than it hurt me. Bill is our personnel director and he couldn't let it go. He ripped into Ryan, which I thought was good— good copy anyway. He said if Buddy were a scout, he would have to write his reports in pencil because he changes his mind so often. He said, "If we win, it's because he's a genius. If we lose, it's because there's no talent there."

Buddy did the same thing to Ron Rivera the year before. It's such a bad deal. It's tearing down what you try to accomplish in the organization. If one thing good comes out of him being a head coach, it's that he can't do that. He cannot do that anymore because he's the guy in the draft room. He'll probably have to have someone tell him who to pick and who to play because it's going to be hard for him to decide who's good and who's not good. It will be interesting.

I had heard of Perry before we went to Arizona in the spring of 1985 to put all the college prospects through tests. I had heard there was a "Refrigerator" and an "Ice Box," who was Tim Newton, the 300-pounder the Vikings took from Florida. Both were defensive linemen, but when I saw Perry run the 40-yard dash, I said to Tobin, "How would you like to tackle that son of a gun?" He weighed 356 pounds and looked like a thundering herd running down the field. Kind of hard to believe. That's when I really got intrigued by him. I said, "Bill,

I really want to analyze this guy." He said, "I'm glad you do, because I like him."

On draft day, Bill and I had our minds made up. Jerry Vainisi and Michael McCaskey wanted Jessie Hester, the receiver from Florida State. That's the only time I ever got mad at anybody. Perry was who I wanted and all of a sudden somebody said no. It would have been different if the draft board was set in such a way that we could have filled a glaring need. But we didn't think we were hurting at wide receiver with Willie Gault and Dennis McKinnon and we thought we had capable backups. If we didn't go Perry, we would go Hester and the Raiders would go Perry. McCaskey and Vainisi wanted to ask Dale Haupt and Haupt wanted Mike Gann, the defensive lineman from Notre Dame. Dale wanted Gann because Buddy Ryan told him he wanted Gann. I said, "Look, you have your personnel guy right here and he wants Perry and so do I." What it boiled down to is we didn't want to play against him. We took almost the entire 15 minutes to decide. We talked to him, talked to his agent, talked to his coaches at Clemson. We talked about his weight and whether he could control it. Finally, we agreed. We did the right thing. We took a lot of heat about it, but we did the right thing, because the guy is a hell of a football player. He's a big man with some fat on. He's not just a fat man. I think people expected to see a guy standing out there stationary on the field and if anybody came near him, he would try to clutch him like a flytrap.

That's not what he is. He's a football player. In his first two games at Clemson in his senior year he was the best player on the field. Then his weight went way up and his stamina went down. The Clemson coaches knew they made a mistake by not controlling him. We thought we could take a chance on him and control him.

I talked to Ryan about playing Perry a little more. He started in the "46" against the Redskins in the fourth game, but he didn't play much in the first five games except a little on kickoff coverage. So I decided to try to give him something to get him involved in the offense. I was trying to motivate him and keep his confidence level up, because he was getting no motivation and confidence built up by the other guy. When I put him in to kill the clock at the end of the 49ers' game, I wasn't getting at Bill Walsh. I really wasn't. I was going to put Perry back there and it just turned out to be kind of fitting, because Walsh had put Guy McIntyre, their 270-pound guard, back there in the NFC championship game the year before. I kind of forgot about using Perry until Johnny Roland, our backfield coach, asked, "You going to put Perry in?" I said, "Yeah."

I had thought he would be good in short yardage and goal line situations, but when I saw that little puff of dust come out of there on the infield in San Francisco, I said, "He's ready; we'll let him go." He really gave you food for thought. I think the coaches enjoyed it. I think they thought I was a little crazy when I brought it up, but then they really enjoyed it. They started making up plays. "We'll let him trap and lead Payton through." We just figured that in 100 years, nobody is going to care anyway. Who was to say it would work out so well?

First of all, it was amazing we would be down at the goal line so often, starting with the Green Bay game on Monday night, October 21. But it worked out. First, he led Payton through for a touchdown and then he scored himself. Then he led Payton through again. Both blocks were against George Cumby and they were awesome. Usually when two bodies hit, there's an impact point and both stop a little bit. When Perry hit, it was just like an earth mover. I didn't know it was going to make him a national hero. Of course, it made us the bad guys in the eyes of the Monday night announcers, but if they say we were trying to rub it in, as a matter of fact, they're stupid. It doesn't make any sense. We put the kid in the backfield because he was going to lead us into the end zone. My goodness, if that's not good football, I don't know what is. Maybe we ought to forfeit and just give the other team the game. We like to play the way it's supposed to be played. All of a sudden, you do something a little bit different and now you're making fun of the opposition. I didn't know we were so offensive. We weren't so offensive three years ago when we were 3-6. People weren't afraid to offend the Bears for years.

The most hilarious thing about this Perry thing was it kind of busted this staid image in the NFL that all running backs are slender, 6 feet, between 185 and 215, and built. He made a farce out of this. Every underdog in society relates to Perry and maybe every person who is a little bit overweight. It's got to make us take a look at this whole darn thing of rating athletes. Guys like Spud Webb can play. He can win the NBA dunk contest and he's only 5-7. We stereotype everything and say, "Nobody can do it but this guy." That's why when scouts come back and tell me about a guy, I want them to tell me first, "Can he play football? Tell me what kind of character he has and how smart he is and then tell me about his size, weight, and speed."

I think it's fun to do things people don't expect to be done or don't really think can be done. To me, watching Perry run over Cumby was as much fun as I had all year. Then we decided he could catch, too, and we put in the pass to him that he scored in Green Bay. He can throw, too. We started working on a rollout pass for him when we went indoors to practice at Morton East high school. We didn't get a chance to use it until the Super Bowl. We had it in for about six weeks. I didn't have it in the game plan for the Rams or Giants in the playoffs, but we put it back in for the Patriots. I thought it would work. I just didn't realize Emery Moorehead would be covered on the play. It was worth a shot. I was glad William didn't throw the ball. It's very unusual for a guy to catch a touchdown, run a

touchdown, and throw a touchdown. We had two guys do it—
Payton and McMahon. Perry would have been the third.

We really stumbled onto something pretty good. I can see
him really being an effective part of our goal line offense from
now on, especially if he comes in at 290 or 295 where he can
really accelerate. It's going to be hard to stop him. It almost
can't not work. You hit him straight ahead, it's pretty hard to
stop him, I don't care what you do. Here's a guy who weighs
over 300 pounds who knows how to run and runs with better
body lean than most running backs. And he likes to do it. He
really gets a big kick out of it. He's agile. You saw him bend
down and pick up a ball on the move and run 59 yards with it
in Detroit. A lot of guys can't do that. There's a lot of things he
can do that a lot of people can't do.

We wanted to get him in more on defense earlier, but we
kept meeting with resistance. Finally, I said we had to put the
best 11 out there and he had to play. That's exactly what I told
Ryan. I don't care who gets the credit. I told him he had to be
out there and he was out there. Against Minnesota in the
eighth game, he played most of the game and kept their quarterback, Tommy Kramer, from stepping up in the pocket and
hurting us like he did in the third game of the season in Minnesota. If you look at the statistics on defense in the first seven
games and the statistics in the last nine games, you will see that
the average per rush for the other teams got lower. In fact, it
went from 4 yards per attempt to 3.4 yards. If you include the
two playoff games and the Super Bowl, it went down to 3.2
yards per rush. He wasn't playing in passing situations and
ended up with six sacks for the year. He also sacrificed himself
a lot on the pass rush for other people. But I'm not going to go
on a crusade for how good a football player he is. I don't care
who thinks he's a good or bad football player. People who
don't think he's a good football player ought to have their
heads examined.

It was important that we helped him get his feet under him. He was playing behind two all-pro tackles in my opinion—Dan Hampton and Steve McMichael. So we moved Dan to end in place of Mike Hartenstine. No slight to Mike; I just felt our best 11 people had to go onto the field. I kept getting this ridiculous argument about Hampton being better inside than outside. Well, he made all-pro outside. The worst part is they almost had him psyched into believing he couldn't play outside. He will play wherever he wants to play. He played inside in the "46" and that was all right.

Perry worked hard and was an ideal citizen. He did everything we asked. He got down from 330 when he reported to 304. The way his year was going at first, he could have been lost in the shuffle. We stopped that. There were a few guys who probably felt Perry got too much publicity. But he didn't plan it. I didn't plan it. It just happened. Early in the year when we had our winning streak going, Perry came along and took pressure off and kept everybody loose. I thought it really helped us. If the other guys want to do it, they should bulk up and be able to move; I'll put them back there. His contract is structured so that he doesn't get all his money if he doesn't make weight. He can offset all that with a few McDonald's commercials, but I don't foresee that problem. If he diets and controls himself and gets back into the weight room like he has to do, it will be interesting. His wife has to help, too. You are what you eat. If you eat everything in sight, you'll be everything in sight. I think he'll be O.K. He's one of the ones who carried me off the field after the Super Bowl. I didn't like that. I was just trying to get to Ray Berry to say hello. But Perry had good reason to lift me. I lifted him pretty well.

XXII

Walter Payton and Other Great Players

I thought Walter Payton was one heck of a tough football player before I came to the Bears. I had great admiration for him because of the way he always gave something extra when he was about to get tackled. I like that. Then when I came here, I saw what an athlete he was and how hard he worked and how strong he was. You see his strength, but you can't believe it. Nobody ever realizes how big he is under there. He plays like he weighs 230. He's the very best football player I've ever seen, period. At any position, period. He's a complete player. He will run, throw, block for you. He does everything you ask. And to play for 11 years with the enthusiasm he has is exceptional. How do you stay on the absolute top level for 11 years? How do you do that? Eric Dickerson of the Rams is su-

per, but if he can play for 11 years, then he'll break all the records. That's hard to do. You have to take a vacation
somewhere and Payton hasn't taken one.

As a pure running back, Jim Brown was something special. They said he didn't block. He used to say he didn't need to
block because wherever he went, someone went with him and
it had the same effect as blocking. He was wrong. It wasn't one
guy; it was two or three. Jim Brown could do whatever he
wanted to do. I thought Gale Sayers, no question, was the best
broken field runner, the best cutback runner I've ever seen.
There are a lot of great football players. Johnny Unitas wasn't
bad. A guy who never got credit as a team player was Paul
Hornung. He kicked it, threw it, ran it, blocked it. I still don't
know how they kept him out of the Hall of Fame for so long.

There are a lot of great running backs, but Payton is a
great citizen as well. I think he's a good person. I think he gives
as much back to the game as he takes out of it. Those qualities
alone would make him something special. If that's not important, I don't know what is. I'm sure George McAfee and
Bronko Nagurski and all those guys did the same thing, but
Payton is a great example to young people and to all people.
You aspire to do something good and you work your butt off
at it. He asks no quarter and gives none.

I try to get the ball into Walter's hands as many times as I
can either running, catching, or throwing it. I don't want to
build an offense around one person, except I'm not stupid
enough to not use the best tool I have as effectively as I can. I
like to run the football. I think you have to. It's interesting to
notice the best teams in the playoffs in 1985 all had good running games—us, the Patriots, the Rams, the Giants, the Raiders. I went back and forth between myself and Ed calling plays
for the first couple years. I get into a rut calling them. If I get
to second and 4, you better bet your ass I'm going to get a first
down running somehow, even if I have to run three times. Ed

might go with a play-action pass on second and 4 and get a touchdown.

People were saying Walter was slowing down at the beginning of the season when teams were blitzing to stop him. He hasn't changed. He made a move in our game in Tampa I still can't believe. You ought to see what his legs do on the film. He planted a leg in front of Hugh Green and then took it outside and ran around him. I guarantee you a normal guy trying to make a move like that is going to pull a groin muscle. You just have to pop something. I mean he was going one way and his legs went woosh, and he went the other way. That was a big-time move.

He never wants to come out of games. When he was going for his record in 1984, he didn't play the fourth quarter of an early game. He didn't like it and the media made a big deal out of it. Here's a guy going for the record and the coach doesn't play him in the fourth quarter in a game that's a walkaway. You're darn right I'm not going to play him in the fourth quarter because he's not going to get the record if he gets hurt. The media took it and ran with it. The media could have just said, "We know Walter. We understand Walter." They could have let it go instead of making a big to-do about it. In my first year here, there were some stories about him not being happy with losing and not carrying the ball as much as he used to carry it. I said at a team meeting, "If anybody has a problem with anything we're doing, come up and see me and we'll try to work it out." He came up and said there was no problem. I don't care whether we run or pass to win. What difference does it make? You try to blend running and passing, but what's important is winning.

In our first game in Minnesota on Thursday night before McMahon came in, O.J. Simpson said a screen pass to Matt Suhey was the most imaginative play he had seen us run in the two games he covered. First of all, I think what O.J. Simpson knows about football I threw up in a bar in Dallas in 1968. I am not an O.J. Simpson fan. Why? Because he doesn't take the time to study the game the way he should, so I don't respect his expert opinion. I don't think he likes me either, so we're even.

I admire a lot of guys for a lot of reasons. I like people who are overachievers, guys who get the job done. The one player who really impressed me the most of all the guys I played with was Roger Staubach. I thought he worked so hard at it. I thought he paid the price and did all the things you were supposed to do. Then I thought when he reached the pinnacle of success, he handled it with great humility. He handled it the way it's supposed to be handled. He gave something back to the public and to the fans. He also provided an image of what was right for youth. He was just a good person. This hits some people wrong, but he was the kind of guy you want your kids to be like.

Those are the people who get ahead in life. They don't have any problems. God didn't create everybody equal in talent. But when you see great talents exhibit the same qualities of effort that others exhibit, that's what makes them great. I don't know that Payton talent-wise is greater than somebody else. Staubach certainly wasn't that great talent-wise. But they took the talent and realized they were going to maximize it. To me, that's ideal. I know if you get those kind of people, you're going to be tough to beat. Mike Singletary is a good example of a guy who has talent and tries to maximize it. Steve McMichael is another good example. We have a lot of guys like that and the more you have like that, the less of the other kind they're going to put up with as a team. They're going to go to the guy and say, "Hey, shit or get off the pot. Do something. Let's contribute. Let's be a part of this thing."

Roger overcame the disadvantage of missing four years of pro football while he was in the Navy. Landry went with Craig Morton originally, which was the right decision because Craig was the better quarterback at the beginning. When Roger came on, he was a leader. He made things happen. The players believed in him. Tom didn't make the decision on Staubach for good until after the 1971 game in Chicago when he alternated Roger and Craig on every play. We lost that game to the Bears and then won 10 straight including the Super Bowl in New Orleans. It was a tough decision for Tom. The fans were laughing. But it was best for the football team to make a decision on one. Tom felt those two personalities would have really split the team. Dan Reeves and I argued for Craig to be the starter. Shows how smart we were. That's why we're coaches.

When you're talking about Pro Bowl players or Hall of Fame players, you should talk about people you played with or against. I played against and with a lot of great linebackers—Mike Curtis, Bill Forrester, Ray Nitschke, Chuck Howley, Matt Hazeltine, Bill George, Joe Schmidt, Dave Wilcox. There are so many. Wilcox was a hell of a football player. He'll probably never make the Hall of Fame, but he was better than most of them in there. That son of a gun could play. If you blocked him, you better pat yourself on the back because he was tough.

I thought the biggest compliment I could give a guy was to call him "pro." One of the ultimate pros I ever saw was Preston Pearson. He worked at it. He was the best I've ever seen at what he did—a third-down receiver. In 1975, we went to the Super Bowl in Dallas basically because of him. He was no slouch as a running back when he played in Pittsburgh. He was a great blocker, cut linebackers down like cordwood. Best deal the Cowboys ever made. He had moves on moves.

I've seen a lot of great receivers. I was thinking if I had to pick an all-pro team how hard it would be, but as receivers I would have to say Charley Taylor and Drew Pearson. I'm not arguing against Ray Berry or Lance Alworth or Don Maynard. I'm just telling you in the clutch, Drew Pearson made more clutch catches than anyone and Charley Taylor was the most devastating receiver, runner and blocker who ever played. Drew would catch the ball and take the punishment. He made the hard catch and the easy catch. He did things that made the Cowboys' whole passing game successful.

Bob Hayes revolutionized the game and showed what speed could do. He made people quit playing man-to-man defense. They had to start playing zones. When he first came up, he was unbelievable. He wasn't blessed with the greatest of hands or the greatest of moves. The Good Lord just said, "You are going to run fast." He took that gift of speed and made himself a good football player. I had to be there when Bobby had to be released. I'm the guy who had to say it. I was the receivers' coach. Tom asked who they should keep. Do you keep Hayes or keep younger guys? I said we had to go with younger guys.

The three best tight ends were John Mackey, Ron Kramer, and Jackie Smith. Everybody said all Jackie Smith had was speed. He was tough, too. He was a hell of a football player. It's ironic that Jackie had such a great career and probably the main thing he'll be remembered for was the pass he missed in Super Bowl XIII against Pittsburgh. That would be atrocious because it has no bearing on what a great football player he was. Rick Casares was a prime example of that kind of athlete. Calvin Hill was like that. He worked at it and had great pride. George Allen said if you hit Calvin, he'll stop running. I thought that was the silliest thing I ever heard, because I thought the more you hit him the harder he ran.

Mackey was probably the greatest runner as a tight end and Kramer was by far the best blocker who every played the position. There are no tight ends in the Hall of Fame. The position wasn't even called tight end when I came up. It was called closed end and P.O. or P.I. for player out or player in. Nobody will ever give Mr. Halas credit for being a great X and O technician, but he did some great things. He utilized a guy who caught only 40 passes in college and made him a tight end who caught 56 passes in his first year, then 58, then 59, then 75. Halas was the one who said, "Ditka can catch and we have some people who can throw, so go ahead and utilize the position." We did things with the tight end before anybody else ever did them. We had the tight end in the slot before anybody else. We flexed the tight end out before people ever did those things.

I don't think about not being in the Hall of Fame. Football doesn't owe me anything. I owe everything I have to football and I don't say that to be a smart aleck. I do try to tell our players that if you play on a good team, you get more recognition.

STRAIGHT TALK

XXIII

Changing of the Guard—'86

I don't know what 1986 holds. I don't really like to deal with the future; I deal in the present. To see our new coaches and the changes we have made excites me because everything that's a challenge is exciting to me. It's a challenge to work with new people and to implement new ideas. To do some of the things on defense that we have always wanted to do here is going to be fun. It's going to be a challenge and it's not going to be easy, but it's going to be fun.

We lost Coach Ryan and Coach Haupt and Coach Ted Plumb—all to the Philadelphia Eagles. Vince Tobin, our new defensive coordinator, doesn't want to be another Buddy Ryan. He wants to be Vince Tobin. He has had excellent success over the years in the Canadian Football League and in the United

States Football League. If you want to talk about statistics, his teams are always up at the top. But statistics aren't the answer; it's wins and losses, and he has the record, too. After he was hired, almost all of our defensive players came up to talk to Vince and tried to get a feel for what he wants to do. As far as I know, they are excited about the challenge and the part they are going to play in the new regime. In the beginning, it's not easy when you change. Change isn't always acceptable or desirable. Change will be acceptable only if we get good results.

I'm sure they're going to test Vince and I'm sure there will be some resistance, but results are what overcomes this. My assistant coaches are an extension of me and I expect them to be treated with the same courtesy that I expect to be treated with. If we find players who think it's too hard or want to rebel, we'll replace them no matter who they are. We've already proven we will do that. We're in a unique position. We have some people who haven't played for us yet who maybe can play as well as some of these guys who think they can't be replaced. We have to have teamwork and communication and cooperation and if I feel it's not there, then I'll make a change accordingly and I won't look back. I never have and I'm not going to start now. I feel everybody will be excited about what we're doing. The one or two who may not be—we just don't have time to wait around and coddle to them. We don't have time to wait for stragglers. We'll just go ahead without them.

We are still going to play tough, aggressive defense. We will still be a team that challenges people. We will give a lot of different looks and we hope we can take the pressure off some of our people by changing up a little bit more than we have in the past. We will play more zone defense. That might help us get more turnovers. We have the right type of athletes to create turnovers. I don't like to see us playing with our backs to the quarterback and that's what happens when you play man-to-man coverage all the time. The linebackers have to turn and run with receivers instead of dropping back into zones. We will play both four-man fronts and three-man fronts and you haven't seen the last of the "46" defense. You may have heard the last of it because it won't be called that anymore. It will be called whatever Vince wants to call it.

We're also going to be radical about where we play some people. We'll have different players in different positions. People might raise their eyebrows, but that's life. If we decide to stand up William Perry and play him at linebacker, then we'll do it; we don't care what people think about it. Or, if we decide we're going to play Perry at end a little bit and play Dan Hampton at nose tackle some, then we'll just see what happens. John Levra is our new defensive line coach. He has a great personality and can relate to the players. I think he'll be able to handle anything that Steve McMichael or Richard Dent or Perry or Dan or anybody else can throw out.

We added Dave McGinnis as our linebacker coach because we really were short one coach. Buddy used to handle the linebackers as well as coordinate the defense. We needed a coach to specialize in linebackers. That will make it easier for Vince to coordinate the whole thing and take time in each of the areas. At age 35, Dave adds a little more youth and vitality to the staff. We were the oldest staff in the league.

Jim LaRue is back to coach the secondary. I've seen more cohesiveness and more togetherness among the whole defensive staff this offseason. Everyone seems to be complementing each other and there is great camaraderie. They seem to be having fun. Sometimes you have to bring new faces into your organization for that to happen. It's not a one-man show and I never meant for the coaches on offense or defense to be a one-man show.

Offensively, we still have to complement the defense, so we have to improve there. Ted was a tough coach to lose because he worked well with our young receivers. But the addition of Greg Landry is really going to help us because it's a two-fold addition. He will help us as a receiver coach because he knows the passing game. And he will help us as a quarterback coach because he played quarterback for 17 years. He knows the best routes and best adjustments for the receivers and what's best for the quarterback. Ed Hughes, our offensive coordinator, has done a tremendous job with our quarterbacks, but this will give him a chance to oversee the whole offense more. He is also going to work more with the receivers. A guy who played quarterback like Greg can help the quarterbacks with their mechanics. I've seen quarterbacks come and go and I know right techniques and wrong techniques, but coming from me it wouldn't have as much meaning as coming from a guy who played the position for so long. We still have Johnny Roland, our backfield coach, and Dick Stanfel our line coach. They are two mainstays who have a lot of input into the game plan. We'll take everything John says, everything Dick says, everything Ed says, and everything Greg says and formulate our game plan. We can't use it all. That's where I come in. But we can incorporate one or two new ideas a week.

Jim Dooley is also a great help as coach in charge of quality control. He was head coach from 1968 until 1972. Mr. Halas rehired him in 1981 when Neill Armstrong was head coach. When I came in 1982, I heard all the rumors about how Halas had hired him to be a spy. I disagree with that. Instead of playing cloak and dagger games, you take people and ask how they can contribute to the staff. Mr. Halas asked me if I could find a spot for Jim and I said I had no problem with that, but I said the spot would be basically as a coach of quality control, not as an on-the-field coach. Jim is very good at analyzing film, very good at analyzing the opposition's defense, and very good at picking up signals from the opposition. He's become a very valuable part of the organization. Just because you might not see eye-to-eye with a person or might not agree with who hired him, you still have to try to make the best of it. You should try to put him in the right spot and create an atmosphere in which he can work instead of spending all your time trying to figure out how to get rid of him. Jim acts as sort of an administrative assistant to me. He funnels ideas to me about what the trends are in the league and how teams are trying to beat certain defenses. He's not good; he's excellent at it. He looks at film of upcoming opponents three or four days before the rest of us look and he can tell you, "Here's what they're playing. Here's the kind of 3-4 they're playing." He can tell you whether they're playing a pressure 3-4 or a contain 3-4 depending on the depth of the linebackers. He can tell me what stunts a team likes to run against certain formations.

We were all rewarded when we won the Super Bowl. Having been the head coach, Jim was rewarded tremendously. When I came here, he expressed to me that he wanted to be a part of it, that he really felt we had the ability to get to the top. I think it meant a lot to him, even though it didn't happen with him at the helm as head coach. He's doing what he does best and doing a heck of a job of it.

Steve Kazor has shown he knows what special teams are all about. There were doubting Thomases, but it is interesting that we led the league in overall special teams play. We got criticized for our poor kickoff coverage, yet we still led the league in overall play.

It was a misconception when I came here that I was going to be the bull in the china shop. What is true is I have no problem relating or dealing with anybody whose cause is the same as mine. My cause was to bring the Bears to where they belong, to bring them to a position of respect in the NFL. It was an organizational effort.

My relationship with Jerry Vainisi, the general manager, is unique. He and I were the only two guys Mr. Halas personally hired. That's a great vote of confidence and I feel very close to Jerry. I am adamant in my belief that he is the best in the business at what he does. He is very knowledgeable in designing, breaking down, and handling contracts. He has a good rapport with players based on honesty and fairness. Most players know that.

Bill Tobin, our personnel director, understands what kind of players I like. And the kind of players I like are the kind of players he likes—players who play the game hard and have commitment and character and the ability to learn. We don't really care about all the numbers being exactly in line. We don't look first at whether they are 6-6, 280. Our scouts—Jim Parmer, Don King, and Rod Graves—are conscientious people who get a lot done. Our scouting staff isn't as big as the staffs of most other teams, but if you look at the recent draft picks who are starting for us, it's really phenomenal.

Michael McCaskey, our president, has done some very innovative things. He has stepped in and said "I don't necessarily agree with the way the league has done things, so I'm going to change and I think these changes are good for the game and will not deter us from being a good football team." I'm talking about the salary structure and the idea of not renegotiating every time a guy has a good year. Signing bonuses and reporting bonuses had become a matter of fact in this league and there's not much reason for most of them. Reporting bonuses are absurd. He has tried to turn incentive clauses into more team-oriented things. Our ticket prices have gone up, but he is trying to present a better product to fans and make Soldier Field or wherever we play more comfortable for families to enjoy.

Whether we admit it or not, we live in times in which we put ourselves into crisis situations every day. If you put yourself into enough crisis situations, you learn to deal with them or you self-destruct. Because of some of the changes we have made, some people are saying Coach Ditka has to prove himself anew. Well, the shoe goes on the other foot, too. All the coaches who left our staff have to prove themselves anew, too. They have to find out if they can work within the confines of their organization like we had to find out if we could work in ours. Change is hard, but change is good if you really believe in what you're doing. If your organization—whether it's a corporation or a football team or a baseball club—is based on one man, then you have a problem. Taking one part out of the puzzle shouldn't really destroy it. It might weaken it a little bit, but in time that piece should be replaced.

People say we have an easy schedule in 1986. We had a hard schedule in 1985 and won 15 games. There are no easy or hard schedules from one year to the next. Who's to say Atlanta isn't going to be the fair-haired boy in 1986? Or Philadelphia? Or Cincinnati? When people talk about easy schedules and bad records, I remind them we had our hands full with Tampa Bay twice, Minnesota once, Green Bay once, and Detroit once. Our toughest games came out of our NFC Central Division.

Every once in a while I think what it means to be champions of the world and I love the feeling. It sounds good and feels good and makes sense. The Bears. Champions of the world. Then I think, "How can we keep it that way?" My mind starts thinking about what we are going to do. "How much time are we going to spend on this defense?" "What is our priority in the passing game?" "What do we work on first?" Then I go to the coaches and ask, "What about this?" "What about that?" "Let's do this the first week." "Let's do that the second week."

Platteville has been a catalyst for our success the last two years and I think our players know that. We're going to go to Platteville again and we're going to go early and we're going to practice hard. Then we have a break by going to London for our game Aug. 3 against the Cowboys. I don't know what that's going to create. It's not going to be a perfect environment, but it's going to be a great situation for those players to enjoy themselves. We can have good meetings and still have a little fun. When we come back, we can go back to work in Platteville.

I don't think I've really enjoyed it yet. I think that's something to save for later. Super Bowls aren't won in one year; they're won over a period of time. The first thing you look at in an offseason is how many guys are working out. How dedicated are they? Has the notoriety become all-consuming? I haven't seen that it has. For the most part, our guys have worked out very vigorously and are very enthusiastic. As a coach, I'll do everything I can to see they have a chance to get on the field, because they have proved to me they want to be on the field. I'm sure I'll have some players say, "I did that last year and I did this last year." I don't care about that, just like the fans don't care about what we did last year. They will care about what we do when we open in September. We'll be judged strictly on 1986 and I think that's fair. I don't really remember 1985 that much. Two days after the Super Bowl, we had the shuttle disaster. That put the whole thing back into perspective. The next day, we had the coaching changes. Then we had bad news on injuries to Dennis McKinnon and Leslie Frazier. Those things got us back to earth in a hurry. The priority no longer is the fact you won the Super Bowl; the priority becomes the upcoming season. As soon as we lose one, people will say, "You bums."

XXIV

Motivation and Management

There were six head coaches in the NFL in 1986 who had experience under Landry either coaching or playing or both—Dan Reeves in Denver, John Mackovic in Kansas City, Forrest Gregg in Green Bay, Raymond Berry in New England, Gene Stallings in St. Louis, and myself. You don't see that off any other staff. It shows you who the coach of the year is, every year. It's not all knowing football; it's knowing the other lessons Tom teaches about people and how to handle them.

Philosophically, I believe exactly like Tom. I believe in a multiple offense and multiple ball-control attack. Keep the defense off balance by changing formations and movement and changing snap counts. That's basic philosophy. Now whether you use a one-back attack or two-back attack doesn't matter. I think you have to use two backs. Dan has gone to almost all one-back. But one thing about coaching is it's no different from running IBM or Chrysler. It's understanding people and being able to get the most out of them. Maybe the way you get the most out of them is by making them really believe in what you're trying to do. If you make them believe it is the right thing and it's important, then you get more out of them.

Lee Iacocca said Vince Lombardi told him that his teams had a feeling of love for each other. I think he meant total respect. It's love in the manner of saying, "We're in the foxhole together. You're not going to leave me. You're going to support me. If a quarterback sack or a penalty happens, you're not going to point to me like it's my fault." The love has to do with sharing the good and the bad and working together as a team. You don't necessarily have to say, "I want to take this guy out and have dinner with him," because you might look up and say, "This is the last guy I want to have dinner with."

Somewhere along the line you have to make them realize that nothing is going to happen unless it's done as a team. Not one thing is ever going to happen. But sometimes people start placing a lot of importance on themselves. A team can't be a good team without great individuals, but it all happens within the framework of a team concept.

You take Mike Singletary, our middle linebacker who held out for more money at the beginning of the 1985 season. He is an exceptional young man for our football team. He has done a great job of refining his talents to where he is one hell of a football player. He was on the field every down. But in any other system, he wouldn't be on the field every down. So greatness often comes with the way you are used in a system. Greatness came to me as a tight end because I played for a team that threw the football to the tight end. Greatness comes to the middle linebacker because we play defenses that highlight and protect the middle linebacker.

A funny thing happens in life and you notice it everywhere you go. All of a sudden, someone is not in a system due to injury or holdout or some reason and the team keeps going. Sometimes it does as well. Sometimes it doesn't do as well. Sometimes it does better. In 1984, Seattle found a way to overcome the loss of a great running back, Curt Warner. In 1985, we found a way to overcome the losses of two defensive starters, Todd Bell and Al Harris. We all think of ourselves as being the most important cog in the machine when really we're all just cogs. None of us is any more important than the other because it won't work without everybody.

There are different ways to motivate. Halas sometimes used reverse psychology. He told Davey Whitsell before the 1963 championship that he didn't think he could cover the Giants' great receiver, Del Shofner. It caused Whitsell to say, "I'm going to have to bust my tail." Landry, on occasion, would involve scripture. He didn't do it that often, but on occasion when he thought it was pertinent, he would. It always made a lot of sense, but Landry and Halas and most successful coaches are able to motivate through results. They said if you did the things the way they wanted them done, you were going to get good results. The proof was in the pudding. They had track records to run with. The players say, "Let's take a crack at it. It might work."

I try to relate to the team what is essential about our plan of attack. Even if you reiterate what you have said all week or all month, you have a better chance of being successful. You might emphasize three things, such as limiting penalties or turnovers or errors. You can't overlook things. If you don't mention them and say, "Well, I'm not going to talk about interceptions and maybe they won't happen," you better bet your butt they're going to happen. You better talk about it. If you miss tackles, they don't go away if you don't talk about it. If you have fumbles, you incorporate it as a major part of your practice and a major part of everything you talk about. Our one big drawback on defense in 1984 was we didn't get enough turnovers. We weren't stressing them. We play a very aggressive style of defense. We attack people and knock the living daylights out of them, which I love. But to get turnovers, they have to be constantly on your mind. Block the kick like Minnesota used to do. You think those things through in practices and meetings. All of a sudden it becomes natural. We led the league in turnover ratio in 1985, by far.

I'm not saying you can't get up in front of the team and make an emotional-type talk about it. But it has to be something they can understand and relate to. You can't say, "O.K., the reason we need to score points is the moon is in the third quarter." They have to see the reason behind it and method behind it. It has to be practical.

I played for some great coaches. Who is to say what greatness entails? But they were all dedicated to what they were doing. I had a high school coach in Carl Aschman who would have been a success as a college coach or a pro coach. Maybe he would have been as successful as Halas or Landry or Lombardi. But he was put into a high school situation to mold young people in Aliquippa. Lombardi showed how a guy could go from high school to maybe the greatest coach who ever lived. Tom is the only coach to stay with one team in the NFL for 26 straight years. That's incredible. Mr. Halas was different, of course. He persevered for over 60 years building a league, owning a team, and coaching it. People can't really understand how hard it had to be for him to wonder where the next dollar was coming from.

In all great people there are certain qualities. Leadership is one and I think you develop that and refine it over the years.

I'm sure in the end, MacArthur was a better general than he was in the beginning. Eisenhower was, too. You learn. I think all those coaches I mentioned were very consistent men in everyday life, not only in football but in life. That's important. You always knew where Halas was coming from. He never threw you a curve ball, unless he was really trying to pull one over on you. You can't have too many peaks and valleys. Another quality is you better be enthusiastic about what you're doing. I never thought Vince had the enthusiasm in Washington that he had in Green Bay. I don't know if that's fact or fiction, but it's my opinion. I know Halas was a Bear through and through. If you cut Landry open, stars would come out. He's a Cowboy. It's the same with every successful coach. They look forward to that challenge every day.

There was a *Sports Illustrated* poll of 200 NFL players who said the coaches they would least like to play for were first, Landry, and tied for second, Don Shula and me. I was flattered. What a great compliment. I don't know why they didn't print the names of the guys in the poll, because I don't want them on my team anyway. They couldn't play for Tom, Don, or me. They're probably lazy asses who wouldn't want to pay the price. I can understand not wanting to play for me, but a guy who would say he wouldn't want to play for Landry or Shula has got to be a lazy bum, because those guys have won and won consistently. Do you realize what kind of loser you're talking about? A guy is either stupid, doesn't like winning, doesn't like extra money at the end of the year for the playoffs, or he's lazy. If a player wants to win, he should have no problem, because that's the only thing I want to do. If he wants to get patted on the butt every time he does something wrong, then he'll have a problem.

There is one thing I can't stand more than anything else and that is blaming others. If a guy can't get it done, he can't get it done. That's life. But I hate it when someone says, "I'm playing bad, but I'm not playing as bad as so-and-so." I'm not talking about so-and-so; I'm talking about you. It's a crutch. It lets you accept mediocrity.

There are certain qualities you look for in people whether you run a football team or a business. You look for people who are committed, devoted, and doing the best job. If you see a guy you know is jacking around, the first chance that comes to choose between him and a guy who is breaking his tail, who are you going to keep? Talent isn't going to matter, either. I'll take the guy who is breaking his butt over a guy with talent in a close situation every time. I may get my butt beat a few times, but in the long run, I'll win because I'll have a guy with more character.

You never have problems with the great ones. The ones who want to achieve and win championships motivate themselves. The guy who worries all the time about whether his contract is big enough, you'll have a problem with him. The great ones, you never have problems. Walter Payton missed the first day of a minicamp to go to a testimonial for Muhammad Ali. I was talking to Landry on the phone and asked him, "What do you do about things like that?" Tom said, "I just fine them and go on." I said, "I didn't fine him. I didn't think it was that important." By collective bargaining rules, we're not allowed to fine anybody enough to make a difference anyway. I think that's wrong. If something is important enough to be done right, why can't they leave it to the discretion of the head coach? I don't think it made Paul Hornung a worse guy when he got fined a thousand bucks or whatever it was when Lombardi saw him in a bar the night before a game. I didn't die after being fined $800 for being out with Doug Atkins after curfew in Baltimore once. I went out the next day and played my ass off. But I was fined $800 when I was getting paid $12,000. I think people should be motivated out of fear of failure. If you condone failing, you'll fail. That's what motivates me. I don't babysit guys like Mr. Halas did. He had detectives following around guys like Doug. I don't know if he had one on me.

I don't think players are afraid of me. I don't think I ever dealt from fear. I have dealt from a position of authority. That's my job and I have the final say on who plays and who doesn't play and on who stays and who doesn't stay. If that bothers them, then they better listen and abide by the rules. But the rules make sense. I knew if we did those things, we would win. I base what I do on good judgement and the fact I've had experience at winning and losing.

The hardest thing is making cuts, because you get caught up in loyalties to people. You get caught up into liking people, which is part of life. You see them every day. You like them. You like their work habits. But when you let that interfere with making a decision on what's really best in the long run for the football team, you have problems. It's like the guy who makes that decision for the corporation and what's best for the corporation in the long run. Is it the guy who has been around and is loyal, or is it the guy who is new but is really maybe a step ahead of the times and is innovative and in the long run is going to be a great asset? Every personnel decision is hard for me. The one that got the most publicity in 1985 was keeping rookie kicker Kevin Butler over the old veteran, Bob Thomas. I made the decision every day I watched them. There was nobody who liked Bob Thomas more than Mike Ditka. But I hope an ability I have is to see the difference between a good player and a player who can become a great player. It's no fun to tell people who have been playing for the Bears 9, 10, 11 years that we're going to keep the other guy. The guy with 11 years experience might be better, but in three months, maybe he won't be better. It hurt me more than anything to see some of the old Bear players go—the Danny Neals, the Dennis Licks, the Doug Planks, the Terry Schmidts, the Jim Osbornes. Some retired; some we had to let go. But it's crazy to say it wasn't the right thing to do. We're not always going to make the right decisions. Hopefully, we won't always make the wrong decisions.

If I ran a plant, I would realize the success of that business was due to the people in that plant. You've got to be people-oriented. You have to understand them, what their feelings are, what their problems are, and what their goals are. Where do they want to go with their lives? You have to try to get into them a little bit. You have to pump them up. The self-worth of the individual is the most important thing he has. Take your self-esteem away and you've got crap. We told our players it's the 45 guys in the room that make it happen. It's not only the superstars or the big guys, it's everybody.

We are a people-oriented business. If I'm a manager and I run a corporation, I want to try to get to know as much as I can about what makes Mike Singletary tick and what makes Dan Hampton tick and what makes Otis Wilson tick and what makes Jim McMahon tick. That doesn't mean I have to go to dinner with them every night. I'm not saying to kiss their ass, but I better understand them. I better be sitting back and analyzing what their actions are and what there reactions to situations are and how they deal with things. Everybody is not the same. Some people maybe think the individual goals are more important than the team goals. Maybe just being part of a winner is the most important thing. Maybe going to the Pro Bowl is a big deal. Somewhere along the line, I better talk to them man-to-man.

Someone told me that Art Rooney, 85 years old, owner of the Steelers, comes into the office often and talks to every person in the office and asks them about their mate, their kids—all by name—how are they doing, what are they doing. He genuinely cares. If you care about your people and they know it, then I think they're going to try to do something about it. If you don't care about your people, if you don't reward them for what they accomplish, then I think apathy sets in. They start saying, "Hey, crap on this guy; he's not for real." I understand people get a dollar paid for a dollar earned, but you better care about them, too.

Iacocca said three things are important to make an organization successful: people first, product second, profit third. Is it any different in football? You have to have people. What's the product? It's how you use the people in whatever offense or defense you run. Then the bottom line is: Do you make money? Or, do you win the Super Bowl? Any manager who doesn't understand the importance of people isn't going to be successful. In our case, it's not only the players; it's the office staff. This is a better office staff now than it was four years ago and it's made up of basically the same people. Why are they better? Because they're caught up in it. They're excited about it. They're a part of it and they like it. People such as Louise Johnson, our receptionist, like to pick up the phone and say, "World Champion Chicago Bears." Four years ago, they probably would have liked to have done it, but they probably couldn't have imagined how it could have been possible.

XXV

Money, Drugs, and the Future

If I were a general manager, I would make Mr. Halas look generous. I would really be tight with the money. The scripture tells us that wisdom is not wasted on the young. I think as a person gets older, he gets wiser about a lot of things.

The question is: How much is enough? I'm not begrudging anybody anything. I'm just saying before you can eat the whole pie, there's got to be a whole pie there. You just can't eat more pie than there is. If the owner bakes one pie, you can't eat two. If he bakes one and a half and says, "This half is for me and nobody can touch it," then you better eat just one pie. It's got to be equitable. I'm not sticking up for either side. I'm saying somewhere people have to come to their senses and say, "This is a good thing for everybody. We can all prosper with this and benefit and we can all leave something behind for some other people 20 years from now." But if we rape it to death right now and greed takes over, there's not going to be anything left.

I don't think you walk in with an agent and a big stick and say you're this and that. It happened to us before the 1985 season. We had several holdouts and played the whole season without Al Harris and Todd Bell. What bothered me was the audacity not so much of the players but the agents saying, "You can't play without our people." Bullshit! We can play without anybody. I don't know how good we'll play but I guarantee you a lot of owners are going to start looking at what we did and say to themselves, "O.K., what are my chances of being 15-1 with this guy or without this guy? I can end up 10-6 without him just as well as with him and I can save myself $500,000."

Sure, we need McMahon, we need Richard Dent, we need Payton, we need Singletary. We need them all. But if we miss one, I don't think we're going to become a bad football team immediately. Early in training camp I told the players at a meeting we could win with the guys in the room. That's before anybody came in. I think a lot of them thought I was full of shit. But I really believed it. I think loyalty is a great thing. I think if you're loyal to people, they're loyal to you. I was loyal to Dave Duerson and Wilber Marshall and they were loyal to us. Both should have gone to the Pro Bowl.

I felt very sad for Todd Bell and Al Harris. Maybe there have been greater moments in Chicago Bear history than the Super Bowl victory, but I never had been a part of one. For somebody to have a chance to be a part of it and let it go by the wayside for a few dollars is something I really just can't conceive. Of all the guys who were holding out at first, the only one I thought we wouldn't get was Bell, because of his agent, Howard Slusher. I thought somewhere along the line Harris would come in. I had rated Todd tremendously high in importance to our team in 1984, because I loved his attitude and the way he played. But Buddy Ryan said there was no way we could line up without him. We proved we could do that. Determined men working together can accomplish anything. I didn't say a determined man. You can't keep losing players. There certainly is a line. You can't spend money scouting players, signing them, coaching them, developing them, and then all of a sudden say you aren't going to pay them anymore. That's probably what bothered Buddy more than anything. But in the case of Bell, I agreed with the club. I thought the demands were outrageous. I don't think either Bell or Harris were more important than I and they were asking six times what I make.

If you stop and look at all the great athletes in history who have never played on a championship team, they would give up a lot of things to wear that ring. But you don't understand that until you do it. In a team sport, the ultimate is what the team does. Now if you're a golfer or tennis player or boxer, you're by yourself. But we're in football and we depend on each other. Everybody has a self-worth; I'm not saying everybody shouldn't go out and get what they're worth. But team success is going to bring them more than they ever thought. There is no greater reward than knowing, as the saying goes, "you're completely spent, you gave your all, you played your best, and you come off the field victorious in a game of competition."

The money you earn and the money you win in the playoffs only lasts a little while. I bet half the players can't tell you where the money is right now. It's gone! But if you have that ring that says you're the best at what you do, isn't that what you want? I know this is corny and idealistic, but I think it's great to be able to say, "Hey, we're the best."

As soon as we won the Super Bowl, I saw that a few players started complaining about how much money was going to

be spent on our rings. We were the same way in 1963. We were
waiting for mink coats for our wives like the Packers got. But it
doesn't matter. The rings will be nice. I saw where Jim McMahon said they will probably come from a Cracker Jack box. If
they don't want them, don't take them. We'll give them to
somebody else. It's no big deal. A hundred years from now, nobody is going to know or care anyway.

Nobody is underpaid in football. There are a lot of people
overpaid, but there's nobody underpaid. I know all the arguments about making the money while you can because of short
careers. There just comes a point where you can't pay $60 for
$1 earned. Players think they're underpaid if there's somebody
somewhere else making more money and playing the same position.

I think you're privileged to play football or play sports of
any kind. If anyone thinks they aren't privileged, then I don't
think they ought to do it. If a guy's not happy, don't do it. Nobody forces you. Go find another job that will pay you
$300,000 a year. Where the hell are they? There are none. They
don't pay street-sweepers or window-washers that kind of
money. We don't pay the President of the United States that
kind of money. This is a kid's game and we shouldn't lose sight
of what we're doing. The NFL is a product designed for the
pastime of the American people. And they foot the bill. When
they decide to quit picking up the tab, we'll all find something
else and there will be an abundance of street-sweepers in the
world.

There are some things I don't understand about contracts,
too. What is a contract? A bond between two groups, two cor-
porations, two people. Why is it signed? To protect both sides.
Who is always wrong about contracts lately? The owners are
always wrong. That is what has happened in sports. Just because the owner is the big guy, he's wrong. When a player signs
a contract, he should honor it. You can't say two years later it's

no good. Be a man about it. I'd like to say my contract is no good. I'd like to better it. Everybody would. But if you play good enough, you should get a better one. I don't care what the players think of my opinion. I worked too hard in the NFL as a player and I know what I made. And I'll tell you what: I thought I earned it. I can't feel sorry for these guys. Maybe that's why I approached Bell and Harris that way. I don't feel sorry for baseball players who make a million dollars and bat .204 either.

Another thing that bothers me is all these personal clauses in contracts. You pay a guy a contract and all of a sudden he says, "Well, if I'm all-pro, what do I get?" If I'm the general manager, I would ask, "What the hell am I paying you the first contract for? If you do all those things, then your next contract would be better." But I shouldn't talk. There's a clause in my contract that pays me more if I'm coach of the year. I fall into the same category.

Reporting bonuses are the biggest joke. You sign a guy, then you give him a reporting bonus for four years. Where the hell is he going to go? To Canada? And some teams pay players extra so they will work out in the offseason. They pay a player to enhance his livelihood. They pay him to allow him the opportunity to make $300,000 a year. You have to pay a guy to do that? It seems asinine and stupid and childish to me. I mean what's going on? Something's wrong. There's a new theory that football owes a player everything. Not so. I'm not begrudging the individuals making all the money, but they act like it's due them. It's not due anybody. They have a God-given talent to use and enjoy. They can make a good living and provide a means to an end. But sports has become an end in itself. There's no more working at Penney's or Woolworth's when it's over. When a kid comes out of college to go into the NFL, it's like a retirement party.

I never had an agent. To me, that's the biggest farce in

football. Why would a guy want to use an agent? I signed
every contract I had personally. There was some fun to that.
You had a face-to-face confrontation. You had enough guts to
sit down and defend your talents. I'm not saying I was right
and everybody else is wrong. I'm just saying that was part of
the fun of it. Maybe some guys are taken advantage of. I'd
have a lawyer now to look at how to structure these new contracts, but I don't think I'd have an agent. I think the personal
touch has gone out of football and sports. I think the agent is
one of the worst things that has happened from the beginning
of sports. The agents pay the players, give them a car in college, take care of them, buy them nice clothes. The athlete really sells his soul to them. I see the agents as people who are unnecessary. They've made a place for themselves that is very
comfortable for them, but I don't see where the great need for
them is. A lot of athletes wouldn't agree.

If football went to free agency like baseball, I think it
would be a mistake. There would be teams that would try to
buy everything and that's a hard thing to do. A team has an obligation to a player and the player has an obligation to a team
for a certain period of time. If you invest in certain players and
develop a team around certain players and all of a sudden
those players are no longer with you, you have to rework everything. The players say just pay them, but not all owners are
created equal. If the 49ers or Raiders want players signed, they
sign them. Some teams say, "Well, we want to win, but . . ."
The 49ers and Raiders don't say "but." When you're competing against that, you're up against something. But it can work.
It worked in Pittsburgh, Dallas, and Miami, where everything
has stayed in balance. I don't say the 49ers or Raiders are
wrong; that's their philosophical approach to winning. It
doesn't always work.

The people playing the game are tremendously important.
The fans who buy the product are the most important. We're

going to price ourselves out of football being a family game.
Baseball is getting the same way. You're talking about at least a
C-note to take a family of four to a Bears' game. A couple of
those a month and a man can't take his family. I see that as a
major problem.

Another thing the fans are going to get tired of is the copout by the athlete who says drug testing is an infringement of
his privacy or human rights. I don't buy that. We're playing a
public game. The athlete has a commitment to the team, the
league, and the fans to perform up to the best of his ability.
Somebody on drugs can't do that. The way the collective bargaining agreement reads, we can ask them to pee in a jar if we
have justification, which means performance level drops off.
But there is no easy way to confront players. It's hard to tell
when they're on something because the ones on it are habitual
liars. The agreement is not strong enough to have any teeth in
it. I say if we think drugs are wrong, let's put some teeth into
the agreement and do it right. If you get off a boat or airplane
to come into this country, they have a right to search you. If
you don't let them have that right, you don't come in. If you
come into the NFL, they should have a right to search you anytime they want to. I just know what's right and what's wrong.
If players are going to argue about human rights, then don't
play. I don't know how many guys gambled back in the 60s,
but I bet you not too many guys gambled after the suspension
of Alex Karras and Paul Hornung for the 1963 season. I don't
understand why you wouldn't want to pee in a bottle every
week if you had nothing to hide.

I think every team in the league has a minor drug problem, including the Bears. We don't put our head in the sand
and say we're perfect. We try to find out what's going on. It
would be foolish to say we didn't know somewhere along the
line somebody didn't turn up positive in a test because they
smoke marijuana. I'd be a liar to deny it. It's society's prob-

lem; therefore, it's not much different in football than it is in society. But in football, you're putting a lot of money into the hands of a lot of inexperienced people. There are other people out there who just prey on these players. They can't wait to get their talons into them. I don't think the problem is as bad as it was three years ago. I think players are being a little smarter and are understanding about it. When they see a Chuck Muncie get busted out of the league, they have to stop and think. I think on certain clubs a few years back, you had some real heavy users. I think they were trafficking drugs and there was a network set up between players on other teams. I think most of that is eliminated. I think cocaine and hard drug use is down. I believe there is marijuana and barbituates being used. Maybe I'm naive. We had a problem with a couple guys on the Bears a few years back and we knew it. We sent them to an outpatient operation. It didn't work and they're out of football. Those things happen on occasion. You try to look for signs—being late, not taking care of themselves. Then you know someone is doing something besides chewing bubble gum.

The thing we have to remember is the consumer is paying for all this. Someday, someone is going to say, "You know, that's a beautiful lake out there. I could go buy a boat and go out on that lake all afternoon on Sunday and I could have enough money to pay for it with the money I save on football tickets." Nobody said that football is the end-all of the world, that is has to be here forever.

XXVI

Family and Golf

I'm no different from anybody else. I'm just a guy going through life. I've always found ways to land on my feet all my life. I've never been the kind to like a 9 to 5 job. If Tom Landry hadn't offered me that coaching job, I probably would have become a brain surgeon. I've been knocked down, out, and over and I've always found a way to get up and do it. I don't think any of it was luck. I think a lot of it was perseverance and I think a lot of it was help from the Good Lord.

It almost seems miraculous that things could work out the way they did. I just think there was a circle I was put through for other people to touch my life and it was incredible. You can't explain some things. I grew up with all those kids back in Pennsylvania and they're probably all scratching their heads wondering, "How the hell is he coaching the Super Bowl team?" We were just kids having fun together. People don't realize that people really don't change; their situations change and it's how you deal with those situations that counts. You adjust to them or you don't. I'm no different in a lot of ways than I used to be. In some ways, I'm better. In some ways, I'm probably worse. But I've adjusted to a lot of situations I've run into in life. By adjusting, I've had a lot of growth.

People don't understand that people who are in the limelight in any walk of life, whether they are politicians, athletes, actors, or whatever, they're just people doing different things from the people working 9 to 5. What we do is written about, talked about, and argued about. That makes us exposed, but we're really still the same people. We have the same problems. We have arguments. We have times we cry, times we're sad, times we're happy. We have friends we like to be with and places we like to go. Nothing changes. We have a life beyond football, but in my case or anybody's case who is in football, the public sees a lot of that life beyond football, too. If we're doing a banquet or a talk, that's in the paper, too.

I don't have a lot of things I like to do, to be honest. I don't tinker with rockets. I like to play golf. I don't read as much as I used to anymore. I used to read a lot. Now I read some. I just don't believe in reading a whole bunch of fiction. I like to read about people who are doers and achievers. I'm a hero-worshipper of people who live in real life, real times, and make real things happen. I wouldn't pay six bucks to see some glamorous star in a movie, either. My hero is not some guy who is playing Tom Mix in a movie. I don't give a damn what he's doing.

A lot of the people who have achieved have overcome things. Start with Babe Ruth. He hit a whole lot of home runs, but he struck out a lot of times, too. Iacocca, Patton, and Reagan are other people who have done it. Most inventions are made by people who had setbacks and disappointments. I believe it's not so much what you do in life; it's what you overcome.

I never really understood my dad all the years I was growing up because he was very strict. He raised us with very strict discipline and didn't let us get out of line. But now I think in retrospect I know why he did it. He loved us enough to try to do the job the best way he knew how to raise us. I'm not saying it was the best way that society would say. Maybe Dr. Spock would have said, "Hey, that's all wrong to raise kids that way." But my dad raised kids pretty damn good. He understood right from wrong. He knew when things were wrong, punishment followed. It was interesting as I got older to see how much my views paralleled his views. I started thinking exactly like he thought. I used to say I was surprised at how much my dad had learned from the time I got out of high school until the time I got out of college. At the age I am now, I have such a great love for him. What he did was unbelievable. When I was growing up, I didn't care if I didn't see him for a month because I was afraid I was going to get my butt beat.

I'm not as good a family man as I should be, no question about that. I got married in college and we had four kids while I was playing for the Bears. Mike was born in 1961, Mark in 1962, Megan in 1964, and Matt in 1966. I raised them pretty sternly for a while, then I really got too lax. But they're good kids. I haven't had any major problems. I wasn't around much. That was a copout. I could have been around if I had wanted to. I found ways not to be around. If I wanted to do something else, I did it. When I was around all the time in the early years, the kids had to abide by the rules, but I was not as strict as my dad was. I got beat with the Marine belt, a cat-o-nine-tails, whatever was handy. I got nailed. Most of the time I deserved it. Probably all of the time I deserved it. I never did that with my kids. I beat them with my hand on the butt. It would hurt me worse than them.

I never pushed my kids into sports. They played every-thing, but I didn't push them. I only wanted them to be good kids. I saw a bit of a problem with my brothers behind me cop-ing with the Ditka name. Ashton played very well. Then my younger brother David didn't play, but that was his choice and he wouldn't have been good at it. People tried to push him to play and that's wrong. I encouraged my boys to play football at early ages, but my oldest boy had an asthmatic condition, so there was no way he could play. I preferred to set the carrot in front of the rabbit and let the rabbit try to catch the carrot in-stead of bringing the carrot to the rabbit. I tried to say to them, "Hey, this is what it's all about. You can go through life and be below average or above average or exceptional."

People make up their own minds what they are going to shoot for, not that they're going to get there. But if they shoot to be exceptional and don't make it, they sure are going to feel a lot better about themselves than if they shoot to be average and don't make it. Go ahead and take a shot at being the best. Be the best golfer. Be the best basketball player. Be the best player you can be. You may not make it, but then the disap-pointment that follows will never be as severe as the guy who says, "I know I'm not good enough. I just want to make the team," and then he doesn't make the team. Now what is he go-ing to do? Then it becomes a greater setback. I believe in goal-setting. People say you have to set realistic and reasonable goals. What is a realistic and reasonable goal? Twenty years ago, to pole vault 19 feet would be impossible. But somebody is doing it now. I don't think there is any such thing as a realistic and reasonable goal. I think the mind is a great thing and I think the will is a great thing and I think if you will something—I didn't say wish for it—if you will it and you're willing to work for it, there's a good chance to make something good happen.

I thought it was important that my kids played and understood what it is to compete; sportsmanship and competition provide good lessons in life. I got wrapped up in hockey as a parent and saw some stupid things—people hitting each other over the head with sticks, parents yelling at kids, "Kill the bum." It was crazy. Mike played when he was a kid in Richardson, Texas. I traveled all over with them. They had an all-star team and we took them up to Quebec City, Canada, for an international Pee-Wee tournament. Teams came from all over the world. Since people in Canada knew about the Cowboys and I was an assistant coach then, they wanted me to throw the puck out. Mike's team played the team from Brantford, Ontario, and its star was a kid named Wayne Gretsky. So Mike played against Gretsky when he was 12 years old and got beat something like 27 to 2 or 3. It was incredible. They scored 10 goals so fast, you didn't know what was happening.

I disagree with parents trying to live their lives through their kids in sports. Present the opportunity to the kid, encourage him and support him, but don't make it a life or death thing. Don't get your feelings hurt when he doesn't like it or he's not a good soccer player or he can't hit a baseball or he's a little bit gun shy to tackle somebody. My parents never pushed me. They encouraged and supported me. They were always in the stands at high school football games making noise like everybody else. They still yell when they come to Bears' games, but they don't understand some of the fans in Chicago. They say they don't make enough noise.

Success in sports can be a strain on a family. One of the things that happens to teams after they win Super Bowls is the divorce rate goes up and so do bankruptcies. Football is time-consuming, but it also throws young people into a different social situation than they are used to and some of them can't handle it. They get exposure to things they never thought about. It depends on how they handle the temptations and pressure. Are you going to do something because nine other guys do? Are you going to go out and pick up a couple girls because other guys do?

Sure, the game is time-consuming, but for the money paid, it's a walk in the park. The peer pressure is a bigger problem. That's basically what happened to me. I had known my wife for a long time. We met in high school. You take people for granted and they take you for granted. We had a situation that could have been worked out and it wasn't worked out because of stubbornness. I felt I got to a point where I was creating more problems than I could overcome even if I was there all the time, because of arguments and things like that. So it became not worth it to me to keep the family in turmoil. We split up. It happened in my last year as a player, 1972, after we won the Super Bowl. We made a run at getting back together when I became a coach and I really thought we would, but it didn't work out. It's foolish to go back in life and say it's somebody else's fault. It's everybody's fault. I'm a firm believer in what you want to work out in life, you can make work out. People have to work together and they have to respect the feelings of other people. The key word in any relationship is respect. They can talk about love and they can talk about anything they want to talk about, but respect is essential. You have to respect other people's feelings and positions and territory. You have to give them room to breathe. That didn't happen in my relationship in the end. I would say that probably 99 percent of it was my fault. I could have avoided it. I really thought I made an effort at one point and then the effort didn't seem like it was worth it. So I went my way. I always said I wish I would have done half the things I was accused of doing. I would have been the greatest lover who ever lived. But that's not a fact.

I met Diana in 1972 after we won the Super Bowl. She came into the place we owned, The Sports Page, with a group of her girl friends. We talked and she came back and we talked again. Then after I was separated from my wife, we started dating. I got divorced and Diana and I got married in 1977. We were married in a judge's office. After the ceremony, I went out and played golf and she went back to work. Crazy.

She has been a tremendous positive influence in my life and I appreciate that. She's down to earth about a lot of things that I feel women should be down to earth about. A lot of them aren't. She doesn't get too wrapped up in all the material things that I see some athletes' wives get wrapped up in. Those things aren't important. She's really solid in that area. We have been a good source of comfort for each other. There were some tough times when things weren't too good and she certainly stood very strongly in my corner. That's important. Diana did a great job with the kids, regardless of what anybody says or thinks. You're never a winner in that position, raising somebody else's children, but I thought she did a darn good job with it. She has been a friend, a mother, and a guardian. All the kids came to live with us and Diana had to play a lot of roles.

She has been an influence in my spiritual life. We both went through the Bible study together and found some direction in our lives. Once you believe, it's like anything else—you better practice. You practice through the way you live, through reading scripture, the way you act, the way you interrelate to other people. We don't always do nearly so good a job as we should. I don't think anybody does. But I think you have to think about it. You have to try to make it work.

I catch myself cutting people off, not that I don't have an interest in them; I just don't have the time to devote to them. You just can't cut people off. I find when I'm having problems, I just cut people off. I segregate myself instead of being involved with them. You have to be involved, to let them help and get their input. I'm more willing to help somebody else than let somebody help me. I have to guard against that.

Sometimes you take for granted that your faith will always be there and everything will be fine. But without making the effort, that's just not a fact. You have to make a real effort to live your faith daily. Nobody is going to do it every day. Nobody is going to do it perfectly. But unless you make the effort, you've got no chance at all. My first year in Chicago in 1982, when we came back from the strike, I really had to take a lot of stock in what was going on. I was getting so wrapped up and getting mad and I had to look back and get a grip on things. The same thing happened in 1983 when I had that broken hand. I don't mind intensity. I don't mind anger at the right times. That's a natural thing. It can happen to anybody. I just think sometimes maybe I do expect too much of people and expect too much of the players. That's when I have to take stock and realize they're no different from me. They all try to do the best they can and sometimes we don't do the best we can. That's all there is to it.

My career is not all-consuming. It's not the end of the world. If I sleep in my office, it's only on Monday nights. I like to spend time at home, but then if I want to go play cards at the club, I play cards. If I want to play golf, I play golf. One thing I don't do is anything halfway. I do it all the way when I decide to do it. Sometimes I go to the golf course early and come home late.

I never played golf seriously until I came to the Bears as a player and joined a club and learned how to break putters and things like that. I was terrible. Then I kept getting better and better. I took some lessons, but most of the guys I took lessons from are dead and buried because of the way I played golf. In Dallas, I played with Dan Reeves almost every day we could play. There were moments I got angry. There were a few clubs airborn. I don't know how many clubs I've thrown in the water. I know it's a lot. I used to break putters and I was good at throwing clubs in the water. They say if you can't afford the game, don't play. One time, I had a cart go in the water on me, but it wasn't my fault. It just accidentally slipped into the water, but the people at the country club weren't too excited about it. I was playing with the Bears and I was in a tournament in Florida. We parked the cart beside the green and came up to putt and evidently the brakes didn't hold and it just went right down into the water. All we did was run over and get our clubs off.

One of my favorite Landry stories happened on a golf course. It was when I was still playing with the Cowboys. I was playing golf with a friend and I chipped to the green with an 8-iron and left the club on the fairway. I never had any cause to hit that 8-iron again until I looked at a par 3 that was coming back close to where I left the club. I knew there were people over there, but you couldn't see over the trees. My partner yelled over, "Did anybody pick up Mike Ditka's 8-iron?"

A voice came back, "Yeah, what about it?"

"Well, if you picked up my 8-iron, I'd like to have it," I said.

"Well, I might throw it right in the lake," the voice said.

"Well, if you throw it in the lake, I'm going to throw you in the lake after it," I said. I was really ticked.

I could hear the voice say, "Tito, how do you think Mike will like playing in Buffalo next year?" It was Tom.

I played with Tom one day and every time I'd hit a bad shot, here was my bad word: "Oh, Good Lord." I must have said it a hundred times. At the end of the round, Tom said, "You certainly have coined a new phrase today: Good Lord." I said it was a good thing he was there so it was not that other Lord I was talking about.

Golf is a humbling game, probably the most humbling game there is. Just when you think you understand it, you don't understand it. It's a great game of competition. You can play it against other people, but you have to play against the game and the course you play. You wonder why the greens-

keeper put the pin over there behind the little knoll where you
can't get to it. I never get tired of it. You can learn about yourself. You learn that you can't do anything about the last shot.
The most important shot is the next shot. A lot of people
worry about the last shot. So what? Hit the next one good. No
matter what you did the last time or what you did last week or
what you did last year, it's not important. Same thing in life.
You have to worry about what you're doing right now. If you
do something good now, you can do something spectacular
when you get on the green or down the line. You can't dwell on
the bad things or the past. I think it's fun, plus it's fun to be
out. I like to be out in the sun. To me, there is nothing prettier
than a golf course. People say they would rather walk on the
beach. I don't like to walk on the beach. I like to get up early
and run on a golf course. I've done that my whole life and I'll
start again now because I can run again. I'll come out and run,
go eat, come back and play it. Sometimes we bet too much
money when we play. That gets out of hand, but I am competitive. A lot of people don't bet beans. I'll gamble on the golf
course and I'll gamble playing gin or a small game of poker.
Other things never interested me. I have no interest in horses. I
stopped in Las Vegas when I went to a Pro Bowl a couple of
times and left everything I had and I haven't been back in
years. Some people bet on everything that's played. We played
cards every night in training camp when I was a player. Halas
never liked anyone to gamble, because in those days if you lost
a few hundred bucks it could bother you and distract from
your thinking.

   I spend some time with charities. Athletes are very fortu-
nate to be born healthy and whole. We have a lot to be grateful
for. I think sometimes in sports we have a tendency to overlook
that because people look up to you. Sometimes you forget to
look down and see what other people are doing. In college, I
went to the hospitals when I was at the Shrine game in San

Francisco. It really made an impression on me. Everybody should go to a hospital once a month. It gives you perspective. All of a sudden you wonder, "I have a problem? My problem is winning a football game. This guy has a problem of whether he can turn over in bed." Or maybe a little girl is never going to see eight years old. People say you do this for charity. Well, charity does that for me. My favorite charity is the Misericordia Home for special children in Chicago. Sister Rosemary and her staff do a great job improving the quality of life for those kids. There are so many worthwhile charities.

Except for golf, I really don't have any hobbies. I love my dogs. Ed McCaskey gave us a Belgian Sheepdog named Bear. We have a Schnauzer and a half-Schnauzer. Dogs are forgiving. They always think you're a good guy. They're always glad to see you. They're glad to see anybody. If they haven't peed on something, they'll pee on you. I have a few old cars, but they're a distraction. I'm not mechanically inclined and I don't know enough about them to really enjoy them. I always had a thing for Packards and I was really trying to buy a 1962 Oldsmobile Starfire. I got a 1961 Starfire that is great. It's probably as good as any in the country. There was some nostalgia involved. I started out with the Bears in 1961. I wanted a 1962 Starfire because that's the car I had when we won the championship in 1963. See, everything has a purpose in life.

There are a million definitions of success. I think it's really your work and how you do your work and what you accomplish from it. You don't have to have all the money in the world to have success. A lot of people say success is money or power or prestige or social rank. I don't believe that's it. I think it's measured by your discipline and the inner peace you have. It's being able to handle little situations, to answer individual questions.

I think inner peace is figuring out who the heck you are and where you fit into the game plan of life. Is the whole thing to beat Green Bay or beat Detroit or beat Minnesota? I think I have those things back in perspective now. You do the best you can with what you've got. After that there's not much you can do. Everybody's not going to like me. I think in the beginning I wanted everybody to like me. I wanted the players to like me. Now, if they like me, that would be fine. If they don't, as long as I'm fair to them, that's the only thing that's important. It doesn't bother me what they say. It used to. It used to bother the heck out of me.

I don't consider myself a success because I haven't done all that I want to do. I'm not satisfied. I didn't say I wasn't happy, but when you become satisfied, you have problems. Show me somebody who is satisfied and I'll show you somebody who is not going to win anymore. After a team wins a Super Bowl, I know the divorce rate goes up and the bankruptcy rates goes up and the injury rate goes up and the number of victories goes down. Players don't think they have to work out and don't work as hard. But it's bad to generalize about football teams, especially this Bears' team. People tried to do that all through 1985, saying, "You can't keep that momentum going week after week." Yeah, we did. "You can't play that good." Yeah, we did. I don't think being No. 1 is by accident. Lombardi said it well when he said you have to pay the price. You want to get to the penthouse? What are you going to do to get there? Hope your father is born rich? You set goals and programs and methods to reach those goals. People say teams don't get back to the Super Bowl. There were teams who went back. They were called the Packers and Steelers and Cowboys and Vikings. It will be a challenge for us to stay up there because all the people who are patting us on the back will be looking to knock us off. But there's nothing wrong with challenges.

Somebody asked if success would spoil me. I didn't see Bill Walsh get spoiled. Tom Landry never got spoiled. Chuck

Noll never got spoiled. It won't spoil me. What it does, it probably makes you hungrier. Now we have to devise better methods and better game plans to stay ahead of the other guy. Besides, I haven't done anything.

I went to a luncheon and a girl came up to me and said, "I know you from television." My nameplate was right in front of me. She looked at me and said, "You're Dick . . . . you're Dick Butkus." Then she looked at my name and said, "Oh, you're Mike Ditka." I said, "He's a lot richer, but I'm a lot smarter." When I retire, I'll go to our new restaurant and nightclub in Chicago and stand behind the bar, retired tight end, little pot belly, baseball cap sideways like the old "Coach" in "Cheers." Or maybe I'll make a Miller Lite commercial. I would be the guy who would run through the wall like Madden, but it wouldn't break. I'd bounce off of it. I'd be in a cast every time I did it. But really, I'm a nice guy. I think everybody's a nice guy to a degree. Hell, I'm nice almost every day of the week except Sunday at 5 o'clock when things didn't go good!

Index